1

כָּל יִשְׂרָאֵל

The Prayers of Our People

By Anthea Canes

Contributing author:
Terry Kaye

Additional activities:
Roberta Osser Baum

Editorial Committee:
Dr. Ofra Backenroth
Roberta Osser Baum
Rabbi Martin S. Cohen
Rabbi William Cutter
Sarah Gluck
Dr. Lisa D. Grant
Dina Maiben
Pearl Tarnor
Dr. Wendy Zierler

Behrman House, Inc.
www.behrmanhouse.com

Contents

The publisher gratefully acknowledges the cooperation of the following sources of photographs for this book: Gila Gevirtz 17; Richard Lobell 34, 36, 50, 67, 68, 80, 89, 92

Book and cover design: Stacey May
Illustration: Pamela Hamilton (cover and story art), Bob Depew (activity art)
Project Editor: Terry S. Kaye

Introduction

Welcome to *Kol Yisrael 1!* You are about to meet Ben and Batya, twins your age. I'm Doug, their pet fish. Join them in their home as they light Shabbat candles, chop *ḥaroset* for the Passover seder, and prepare macaroni and cheese for a food drive. With Ben and Batya, you will learn how to start your day with a smile by reciting a blessing when you wake up.

Other blessings will help you turn ordinary moments into special ones. You will learn how to become a partner with God by feeding the hungry and why we recite a blessing—בִּרְכַּת הַמָּזוֹן—*after* we have eaten. Yup, you'll learn *sooo* much that you will even solve the mystery of what's inside a mezuzah case!

There's lots more you'll learn, including Jewish values such as הַכְנָסַת אוֹרְחִים (welcoming guests into your home) and why Abraham and Sarah were the ultimate hosts—Abraham even offered guests water to wash their feet!

You will peek inside the Torah to see where many of our prayers come from and, in every chapter, by solving a "Clue to Cyberspace," you can play a game on your computer.

Finally, you, Ben, and Batya will learn how you can add to your family's שְׁלוֹם בַּיִת—peace, love, and respect in the home. (Don't worry, I'll be at your side, helping you to become a real pro.) At night, before drifting off to sleep, you can feel terrific about all you have learned and all the good you have done!

Batya likes to get up early in the morning. Ben is a night owl. He loves to stay up late and sleep in as long as he can. When *you* wake up in the morning:

What is the first thing you see?

What is the first thought you have

   a) on a weekday? _____

   b) on the weekend? _____

Perhaps the first thing you see in the morning are the numbers on your buzzing alarm clock or your mom or dad shaking you awake. Maybe you say, "Please let me sleep." On the weekends, you may say, "Great, I don't have to get up," as you snuggle under the covers and fall back to sleep.

Describe two favorite activities that make you want to get out of bed in the morning.

① _____

② _____

Now think of a reason you may not want to get up.

Reading Rounds

Read each line aloud.

1. אַ בָּ בַ גֶּ דָ הַ

2. וְ זָ חַ חִ יָ יְ כֶּ כַ דְּ לוּ

3. מֶ ם נ ן ס סְ עֹ פֵּ פִּ פ

4. צוֹ ץ קֹ רֶ שַׁ שַׂ תּוֹ תֶ

Connect the letters below that sound similar.

ע	כ
ק	א
ט	שׂ
ח	ת
ס	כּ

Practice reading the following word parts from the prayer you will learn on the next page.

1. דֶ דָ מוֹ אַ ל אֱ מֶ נִי פָ וְ לֶ ךָ זַ

2. בִּי דֶה נֶיךָ לֶךְ יָם נְשׁ בָּה תִי לָה

Rise and Shine

When we wake up in the morning, we thank God for the strength that our night's rest has brought us, for helping our mind and body to grow, and for the gift of a new day.

Jewish tradition gives us a way to say thank you to God in the morning—with the מוֹדֶה אֲנִי prayer. (Boys and men begin the prayer with the word מוֹדֶה and girls and women begin it with מוֹדָה.)

Practice reading מוֹדֶה/מוֹדָה אֲנִי aloud.

Boys and men say:

1. מוֹדֶה אֲנִי לְפָנֶיךָ מֶלֶךְ חַי וְקַיָּם

2. שֶׁהֶחֱזַרְתָּ בִּי נִשְׁמָתִי בְּחֶמְלָה רַבָּה אֱמוּנָתֶךָ.

Girls and women say:

1. מוֹדָה אֲנִי לְפָנֶיךָ מֶלֶךְ חַי וְקַיָּם

2. שֶׁהֶחֱזַרְתָּ בִּי נִשְׁמָתִי בְּחֶמְלָה רַבָּה אֱמוּנָתֶךָ.

1. *I give thanks to You, living and everlasting Ruler,*
2. *who has graciously returned my soul to me. Great is Your faithfulness!*

Prayer Words

Practice reading these words from אֲנִי מוֹדָה/מוֹדֶה.

thank, give thanks (for a boy or man)	מוֹדֶה
thank, give thanks (for a girl or woman)	מוֹדָה
I	אֲנִי
ruler, king	מֶלֶךְ
living	חַי

Create your own "thank you" blessing for when you wake up in the morning.

Thank you, God, for _____

Odd Word Out

Underline the words that do not belong in אֲנִי מוֹדָה/מוֹדֶה.

○ Circle the first letter of the first word that does not belong.

☐ Box the second letter of the second word that does not belong.

△ Draw a triangle around the third letter of the third word that does not belong.

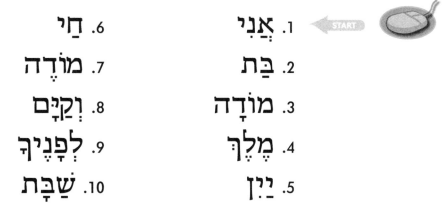

6. חַי		1. אֲנִי	START
7. מוֹדֶה		2. בַּת	
8. וְקַיָּם		3. מוֹדָה	
9. לְפָנֶיךָ		4. מֶלֶךְ	
10. שַׁבָּת		5. יַיִן	

Challenge: Put the three Hebrew letters in the correct shapes below. Then use this Hebrew word (it means "house") as the combination to unlock the closet when you complete the "Clean the Closet" activity in Level 1—מוֹדָה/מוֹדֶה אֲנִי—on your computer.

△ ☐ ○

This is your combination.

Language Link

Look again at the first word of the מוֹדֶה/מוֹדָה אֲנִי prayer.

"Thank" (for a boy or man)   מוֹדֶה

"Thank" (for a girl or woman)   מוֹדָה

We all say "Please" and "Thank you" when we ask for things, and when we receive them. In Hebrew, we say בְּבַקָשָׁה ("please") and תּוֹדָה ("thank you").

מוֹדֶה and מוֹדָה are in the same word family as תּוֹדָה.

In English, ask a classmate for something. Add בְּבַקָשָׁה to your request. For example, you could say, "Pass me a pencil, בְּבַקָשָׁה." Don't forget to say תּוֹדָה when you receive it!

Fill in the correct word—בְּבַקָשָׁה or תּוֹדָה—next to each cartoon below.

_____ .2   _____ .1

Putting It in ConTEXT

Many Jewish practices have their roots in the Torah. For example, the Torah tells us that Abraham got up early in the morning to go "to the place where he had stood before God." From these words, the ancient rabbis explain, we learn we should pray in the morning. Some people pray at home in the morning; some pray in the synagogue.

Now read the words about Abraham from the Torah.

וַיַּשְׁכֵּם אַבְרָהָם בַּבֹּקֶר אֶל-הַמָּקוֹם
אֲשֶׁר-עָמַד שָׁם אֶת-פְּנֵי יְיָ.

And Abraham rose early in the morning to the place
where he had stood before God.
(Genesis 19:27)

Underline Abraham's Hebrew name.

Partner Talk

Discuss with a partner: Jewish tradition teaches us to say "thank you" to God every morning for the gift of a new day. How can seeing each day as a gift and saying thanks help you enjoy the day?

Who in your family can you thank? How can saying "thanks" add *shalom*, peace, in your home?

Clue to Cyberspace

Climb up the first ladder and down the second by reading each word aloud. Then listen to a classmate while he or she climbs up and down the ladders by reading each word aloud.

②	①
מֶלֶךְ	לְפָנֶיךָ
חַי	אֲנִי
וְקַיָּם	מוֹדָה

Now solve the following riddle. The answer, which is one of the words on the ladder, will help you score bonus points when you play the "Fish Tales" game in Level 1—מוֹדֶה/מוֹדָה אֲנִי—on your computer.

Riddle:

It's not my ear and it's not my nose. And it's not you. It's me!

Write your answer in English here. _____

Now write the Hebrew word that means the same thing. _____

Dad and Batya follow a recipe when they bake fudge brownies. The recipe reminds them of the ingredients they need. How do you remind yourself about important tasks you have to do? Do you keep a homework planner? Do you post notes around your desk? Perhaps you ask your mom or dad to be your "memory."

When do you need reminders? What kind of reminders work best for you?

Our tradition offers us daily reminders, בְּרָכוֹת (plural of בְּרָכָה, "blessing"), that allow us to turn ordinary events—eating bread, seeing a sunset, putting on new shoes—into special ones. When we say בְּרָכוֹת, we are saying "Thank You, God, for Your gifts."

Reading Rounds

Practice reading the following word parts and words.

1. בָּ   רוּךְ   בָּרוּךְ

2. אַ   תָּה   אַתָּה

3. אֱ   לֹ   הֵי   נוּ   אֱלֹהֵינוּ

4. מֶ   לֶךְ   מֶלֶךְ

5. הָ   עוֹלָם   הָעוֹלָם

Blessing Formula

In your math class you may have learned how formulas can help you solve math problems. People using the same formula anywhere in the world will arrive at the same solution.

Write a math formula here. _____

Most בְּרָכוֹת begin with the same six words, sometimes called "the blessing formula."

Practice reading the first six words in a blessing.

בָּרוּךְ אַתָּה יְיָ אֱלֹהֵינוּ מֶלֶךְ הָעוֹלָם

Praised are You, Adonai our God, Ruler of the world

Why do you think we call these six words a blessing *formula*? How can a blessing formula be helpful?

_____

_____

In what ways can your family cooperate to bake the yummiest brownies?

Figure the Formula

Number the words below in the correct order of the blessing formula.

◯	◯	◯	◯	◯	◯
אַתָּה	אֱלֹהֵינוּ	הָעוֹלָם	בָּרוּךְ	יְיָ	מֶלֶךְ

God's Menu

Plan what you will eat today by choosing one type of bread, one vegetable, one fruit, one dessert, and grape juice. Circle your choices. Then practice saying the blessing for each type of food.

1. בָּרוּךְ אַתָּה, יְיָ אֱלֹהֵינוּ, מֶלֶךְ הָעוֹלָם, הַמּוֹצִיא לֶחֶם מִן הָאָרֶץ.

Praised are You, Adonai Our God, Ruler of the world, who brings forth bread from the earth.

2. בָּרוּךְ אַתָּה, יְיָ אֱלֹהֵינוּ, מֶלֶךְ הָעוֹלָם, בּוֹרֵא פְּרִי הָאֲדָמָה.

Praised are You, Adonai Our God, Ruler of the world, who creates the fruit of the earth (vegetables).

3. בָּרוּךְ אַתָּה, יְיָ אֱלֹהֵינוּ, מֶלֶךְ הָעוֹלָם, בּוֹרֵא פְּרִי הָעֵץ.

Praised are You, Adonai Our God, Ruler of the world, who creates the fruit of the tree.

‏4. בָּרוּךְ אַתָּה, יְיָ אֱלֹהֵינוּ, מֶלֶךְ הָעוֹלָם, בּוֹרֵא מִינֵי מְזוֹנוֹת.

Praised are You, Adonai Our God, Ruler of the world, who creates different kinds of foods.

‏5. בָּרוּךְ אַתָּה, יְיָ אֱלֹהֵינוּ, מֶלֶךְ הָעוֹלָם, בּוֹרֵא פְּרִי הַגָּפֶן.

Praised are You, Adonai Our God, Ruler of the world, who creates the fruit of the vine.

Did You Know? If you were to eat all of these foods, including bread, at one meal, the blessing for bread would thank God for *all* the foods at that meal.

Why do you think the blessing for bread covers all the foods at a meal that includes bread?

_____

_____

Prayer Words

Practice reading these words from בְּרָכוֹת.

blessed, praised	בָּרוּךְ
you (for a boy or man)	אַתָּה
the world	הָעוֹלָם
bread	לֶחֶם
earth	אֲדָמָה
fruit, fruits	פְּרִי, פֵּרוֹת
tree	עֵץ

 You're an Artist!

Choose four Hebrew words from the list above and write them on the lines below. Then draw a picture to illustrate each.

At the Root

Most Hebrew words are built on **roots**. A root usually consists of three letters that form the foundation for related words. Hebrew roots have no vowels.

The root of בָּרוּךְ is ברכ (כ looks like this at the end of a word: ך). Words with the root ברכ have **bless** or **praise** as part of their meaning. בָּרוּךְ shares a common root with the Hebrew word, בֶּרֶךְ, "knee." בָּרוּךְ reminds us that blessing or praising Adonai is like kneeling in front of a ruler. When we say a בְּרָכָה, it is as if we are kneeling before God.

Read aloud the words below. Underline the words that are built on the root ברכ. Then circle the three root letters in each of those words.

בְּרָכָה   פֵּרוֹת   בָּרוּךְ   בְּרָכוֹת   מוֹדֶה

A Secret Word

If the blessing ending in each line below matches the food item in that line, circle the letter in the כֵּן ("yes") column. If the blessing does not match the food, circle the letter in the לֹא ("no") column.

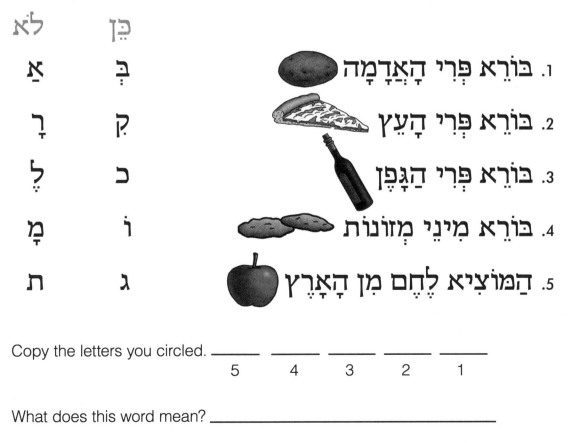

לֹא	כֵּן		
אַ	בְּ	בּוֹרֵא פְּרִי הָאֲדָמָה	.1
רְ	קְ	בּוֹרֵא פְּרִי הָעֵץ	.2
לְ	כ	בּוֹרֵא פְּרִי הַגָּפֶן	.3
מָ	וֹ	בּוֹרֵא מִינֵי מְזוֹנוֹת	.4
ת	ג	הַמּוֹצִיא לֶחֶם מִן הָאָרֶץ	.5

Copy the letters you circled. _____ _____ _____ _____ _____

                                            5   4   3   2   1

What does this word mean? _____

Amen!

Challenge: The word אָמֵן is built on the root letters אמנ (**believe** or **have faith**). Note: נ looks like this at the end of a word: ן. The word אֱמוּנָה, "faith," comes from the same root. אָמֵן is the group's or congregation's way of saying "we agree with your בְּרָכָה." Can you find *another* Hebrew word in the cartoon that is built on the root אמנ? Draw a rectangle around it.

Picture Perfect

Draw a picture frame around the pictures that match the blessing ending in each row. Then recite each complete blessing aloud.

בָּרוּךְ אַתָּה יְיָ אֱלֹהֵינוּ מֶלֶךְ הָעוֹלָם...

1. הַמּוֹצִיא לֶחֶם מִן הָאָרֶץ.

2. בּוֹרֵא פְּרִי הָעֵץ.

3. בּוֹרֵא פְּרִי הַגָּפֶן.

4. בּוֹרֵא פְּרִי הָאֲדָמָה.

5. בּוֹרֵא מִינֵי מְזוֹנוֹת.

בּוֹרֵא מִינֵי מְזוֹנוֹת

Language Link

Read the items below. Do you recognize these foods?

1. תֵּה   פֶּפְּסִי   פִּיצָה   בָּנָנָה

2. לִימוֹנָדָה   פְלֵיקְס   קוֹרְן   פּוֹפְּקוֹרְן

3. קוֹלָה   קוֹקָה   סְפַּגֶטִי   קָפֶה

In Hebrew, write your favorite food from the words above. _____

Now write your favorite drink. _____

Musical Moments

Use your fingers to play the piano as you read the sounds of the letters in the *alef-bet*.

Now play backward from the end of the *alef bet*!

Fluent Reading

Practice reading the lines below. Underline the blessing formula in each line.

1. בָּרוּךְ אַתָּה, יְיָ אֱלֹהֵינוּ, מֶלֶךְ הָעוֹלָם, אֲשֶׁר בִּדְבָרוֹ מַעֲרִיב עֲרָבִים.

2. בָּרוּךְ אַתָּה, יְיָ אֱלֹהֵינוּ, מֶלֶךְ הָעוֹלָם, אֲשֶׁר נָתַן לָנוּ תּוֹרַת אֱמֶת.

3. בָּרוּךְ אַתָּה, יְיָ אֱלֹהֵינוּ, מֶלֶךְ הָעוֹלָם, יוֹצֵר אוֹר וּבוֹרֵא חֹשֶׁךְ, עֹשֶׂה שָׁלוֹם וּבוֹרֵא אֶת הַכֹּל.

4. בָּרוּךְ אַתָּה, יְיָ אֱלֹהֵינוּ, מֶלֶךְ הָעוֹלָם, אֲשֶׁר בָּחַר בִּנְבִיאִים טוֹבִים.

5. בָּרוּךְ אַתָּה, יְיָ אֱלֹהֵינוּ, מֶלֶךְ הָעוֹלָם, גָּאַל יִשְׂרָאֵל.

Clue to Cyberspace

Rabbi Meir said: Everyone should say one hundred blessings a day.

How many blessings would that be in the month of October? _____

Use this clue to score bonus points in "Ben's Skateboarding Street Course" in Level 2—בְּרָכוֹת—on your computer.

Ben and Batya are doing their homework in the study. Ben is lying on the floor; Batya likes to work at the desk.

Where do you do your homework?

_____

Though Batya has seven more algebra problems to complete, she helps Ben do research for his history project. "Thanks, sis," says Ben, "you did a mitzvah. I owe you."

A מִצְוָה (plural, מִצְוֹת) is a commandment in the Torah. Some מִצְוֹת teach us how to behave toward God and to worship God through ritual actions—for example, to believe in only one God and to sit in a sukkah on Sukkot. Other מִצְוֹת teach us how to behave toward other people—for example, to give tzedakah, visit a friend or relative in the hospital, and not steal. That's why, for many people—including Ben—the word מִצְוָה has come to mean "a good deed."

Describe a mitzvah you performed during the last week or two that showed you know how to behave toward other people.

_____

_____

How did performing that mitzvah help make you part of the Jewish community?

_____

Reading Rounds

Sometimes the letter vav looks like this: וֹ

It looks as if it should say "oh" (טוֹ בּוֹ קוֹ). However, וֹ has the sound "vo" if it follows a letter that already *has* a vowel.

Practice reading the following word parts and words.

1. עֲוֹ מִצְוֹ עֹו צֹו עוֹלָם

2. קְ דְּ שָׁ נוּ קִדְּשָׁנוּ

3. בְּ מִצְוֹ תָיו מִצְוֹתָיו בְּמִצְוֹתָיו

4. רָצוֹן צוֹרֶךְ עֲווֹנָה אַרְצוֹת

5. מַצוֹת מִצְוֹת מִצְוַת מִצִּיוֹן מִצְרַיִם

Word Find

Find and circle the word for "commandments" in the string of letters below.

פְּרִילוֹמֶדֲאַדָמָהבְּרָכָהַמִצְוֹתמוֹדֶהַמֶּלֶךְ

Now find and circle "thank you."

הַמוֹצִיאַתוֹדָהַבְּבַקָשָׁהַאֲנִיחַישַׁבָּתבָּרוּךְ

It's a Mitzvah!

When doing some מִצְוֹת—like studying Torah, lighting Shabbat candles, blowing the shofar on Rosh Hashanah, or sitting and eating in a sukkah—we say a blessing. We call such blessings בְּרָכוֹת שֶׁל מִצְוָה (blessings over the commandments).

Almost every בְּרָכָה שֶׁל מִצְוָה begins with the same ten words. Practice reading these words.

בָּרוּךְ אַתָּה, יְיָ אֱלֹהֵינוּ, מֶלֶךְ הָעוֹלָם,
אֲשֶׁר קִדְּשָׁנוּ בְּמִצְוֹתָיו וְצִוָּנוּ

Praised are You, Adonai our God, Ruler of the world,
who makes us holy with commandments and commands us

When we recite a בְּרָכָה שֶׁל מִצְוָה, we add four words to the original six-word formula we learned in Chapter 2.

אֲשֶׁר קִדְּשָׁנוּ בְּמִצְוֹתָיו וְצִוָּנוּ

who makes us holy with commandments and commands us

Draw a line to connect the ten words of the blessing in the correct order and discover a hidden picture.

Blessing Circle

Form a circle with your classmates. Decide which of you will begin the game. The first person says the word בָּרוּךְ, the second person says בָּרוּךְ אַתָּה, the third person says בָּרוּךְ אַתָּה יְיָ, and so on. Continue until you have completed the ten-word formula that begins every בְּרָכָה שֶׁל מִצְוָה. Then have someone else start and see how fast you can say the formula this time. Go on, do it a third time, too!

At the Root

We've already learned that most Hebrew words are built on roots.

The root of קִדְּשָׁנוּ is קדש. Words with the root קדש have **holy** or **set apart** as part of their meaning.

Circle the root letters קדש in each of the Hebrew words or phrases below.

3. בֵּית הַמִּקְדָּשׁ   2. אֲרוֹן קֹדֶשׁ   1. קִדְּשָׁנוּ

The Holy Temple   Holy Ark   makes us holy

5. קִדּוּשִׁין   4. קִדּוּשׁ

Jewish marriage ceremony   Kiddush

Why do you think the Jewish marriage ceremony has "holy" as its root?

_____

Circle the word(s) built on the root קדש in each prayer sentence below.

1. אַתָּה קִדַּשְׁתָּ אֶת יוֹם הַשְּׁבִיעִי לִשְׁמֶךָ.

2. וַיְבָרֶךְ אֱלֹהִים אֶת יוֹם הַשְּׁבִיעִי וַיְקַדֵּשׁ אוֹתוֹ.

3. קָדוֹשׁ קָדוֹשׁ קָדוֹשׁ יְיָ צְבָאוֹת.

Putting It in ConTEXT

עֵץ חַיִּים הִיא לַמַּחֲזִיקִים בָּהּ

The Torah is a tree of life to those who hold fast to it.
(Proverbs 3:18)

We sing these words when we return the Torah to the Ark after the Torah reading. The wise Torah scholar, Rabbi Abraham Isaac Kook, taught that studying the Torah is like planting seeds within ourselves that grow and fill us with life.

Draw a picture of a tree over the Hebrew word for "tree" at the top of the page.

Think of your own comparison for studying the Torah. Complete the following:

Studying the Torah is like _____

When we study the Torah, we first say a בְּרָכָה שֶׁל מִצְוָה.

Practice reading the בְּרָכָה.

בָּרוּךְ אַתָּה, יְיָ אֱלֹהֵינוּ, מֶלֶךְ הָעוֹלָם, אֲשֶׁר קִדְּשָׁנוּ בְּמִצְוֹתָיו וְצִוָּנוּ לַעֲסוֹק בְּדִבְרֵי תוֹרָה.

Praised are You, Adonai our God, Ruler of the world, who makes us holy with commandments and commands us to engage in the study of Torah.

Leaf Lineup

Put the בְּרָכָה in the correct order by numbering the leaves 1–13.

קִדְּשָׁנוּ

וְצִוָּנוּ

בְּמִצְוֹתָיו

אַתָּה

הָעוֹלָם

לִי

אֲשֶׁר

מֶלֶךְ

אֱלֹהֵינוּ

תוֹרָה

לַעֲסוֹק

בָּרוּךְ

בְּדִבְרֵי

Tic-Tac-Toe

Play Tic-Tac-Toe with a classmate. Take turns reading a word. If you are correct, lightly write an X or an O in pencil in that box.

לַעֲסוֹק	אֲשֶׁר	עֵץ	מֶלֶךְ	אַתָּה	יְיָ
וְצִוָּנוּ	הָעוֹלָם	אַתָּה	אֲנִי	בְּמִצְוֹתָיו	אֲשֶׁר
קִדְּשָׁנוּ	מוֹדֶה	אֱלֹהֵינוּ	חַי	אֲדָמָה	אַתָּה

Putting It in ConTEXT

וּכְתַבְתָּם עַל-מְזֻזוֹת בֵּיתֶךָ וּבִשְׁעָרֶיךָ.

*You shall write them (the commandments) upon the doorposts
of your house and upon your gates.*
(Deuteronomy 6:9)

We fulfill this commandment by placing the words of the שְׁמַע and וְאָהַבְתָּ prayers, written on a piece of parchment, inside a מְזוּזָה on our doorposts.

Practice reading the בְּרָכָה that we say when we affix a מְזוּזָה to a doorpost.

בָּרוּךְ אַתָּה, יְיָ אֱלֹהֵינוּ, מֶלֶךְ הָעוֹלָם, אֲשֶׁר קִדְּשָׁנוּ
בְּמִצְוֹתָיו וְצִוָּנוּ לִקְבֹּעַ מְזוּזָה.

*Praised are You, Adonai our God, Ruler of the world, who makes us holy with
commandments and commands us to affix the mezuzah.*

Practice reading these words from בְּרָכוֹת שֶׁל מִצְוָה.

makes us holy	קִדְּשָׁנוּ
with God's commandments	בְּמִצְוֹתָיו
and commands us	וְצִוָּנוּ
to engage	לַעֲסוֹק
in the words of	בְּדִבְרֵי
Torah	תּוֹרָה
to affix	לִקְבֹּעַ
mezuzah	מְזוּזָה

Picture It

Draw two pictures of yourself:

1. **Hanging a mezuzah.** Write the two appropriate Hebrew words from "Prayer Words" on the lines below your drawing.

2. **Studying Torah.** Write the three appropriate Hebrew words.

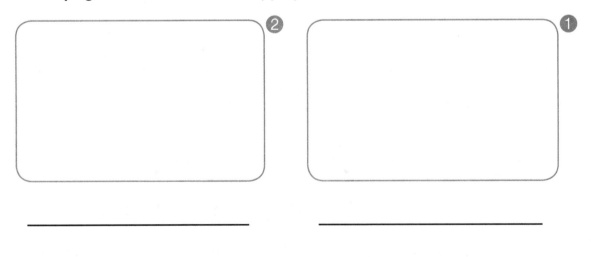

_____   _____

_____   _____

_____

Book Search

Write the English meaning for the Hebrew word(s) on each book below.

תּוֹרָה

_____

מְזוּזָה

_____

קִדְּשָׁנוּ

_____

מוֹדֶה

_____

מִצְוֹת

_____

בָּרוּךְ אַתָּה

_____

Clue to Cyberspace

Read each statement below. If it is True, put a 1 on the blank line next to it. If it is False, put a 0. Add up the numbers. That's the clue to scoring bonus points in the "Ping Pong" game in Level 3—בְּרָכוֹת שֶׁל מִצְוָה—on your computer.

True = 1   False = 0

1. A מְזוּזָה contains the words of the שְׁמַע and וְאָהַבְתָּ. _____

2. בְּרָכוֹת שֶׁל מִצְוָה begin with a ten-word formula. _____

3. קָדוֹשׁ means "holy." _____

4. הַמּוֹצִיא לֶחֶם מִן הָאָרֶץ thanks God for wine. _____

5. The Torah is compared to a tree of life. _____

Total _____

Ben and Batya are excited to receive a wedding invitation in the mail. After a week of school, sports, homework, and chores, they have this special event to look forward to.

You are invited to take time out of your busy schedule to
join us at the marriage of a unique couple

כַּלָּה

Shabbat
who will be married to

חָתָן

Israel and Jewish people around the world

Date: Friday evening through Saturday night
Time: Friday, Sunset
Place: All Jewish Homes
Come refresh yourself and restore your spirit! No RSVP required.

The Marriage Match

Jewish tradition teaches us that just as a חָתָן welcomes a כַּלָּה, so do Israel and the Jewish people welcome Shabbat.

Why do you think Shabbat is compared to a כַּלָּה?

_____

Do you think this is a good comparison? Why or why not?

At the Shabbat table, Ben and Batya and their family say three בְּרָכוֹת to welcome Shabbat.

They light candles to bring the light of Shabbat into their home. Practice reading the בְּרָכָה.

1. בָּרוּךְ אַתָּה, יְיָ אֱלֹהֵינוּ, מֶלֶךְ הָעוֹלָם, אֲשֶׁר קִדְּשָׁנוּ בְּמִצְוֹתָיו וְצִוָּנוּ לְהַדְלִיק נֵר שֶׁל שַׁבָּת.

1. Praised are You, Adonai our God, Ruler of the world, who makes us holy with commandments and commands us to light the Shabbat candles.

They say a blessing to God for creating wine and thank God for taking us out of Egypt and making us free so that we can celebrate Shabbat. Practice reading the בְּרָכָה over wine.

2. בָּרוּךְ אַתָּה, יְיָ אֱלֹהֵינוּ, מֶלֶךְ הָעוֹלָם, בּוֹרֵא פְּרִי הַגָּפֶן.

2. Praised are You, Adonai our God, Ruler of the world, who creates the fruit of the vine.

They say a blessing to God over ḥallah to remember that we are partners with God in creating food. Practice reading the בְּרָכָה.

3. בָּרוּךְ אַתָּה, יְיָ אֱלֹהֵינוּ, מֶלֶךְ הָעוֹלָם, הַמּוֹצִיא לֶחֶם מִן הָאָרֶץ.

3. Praised are You, Adonai our God, Ruler of the world, who brings forth bread from the earth.

Which בְּרָכָה above is a בְּרָכָה שֶׁל מִצְוָה? Write the number. _____

Prayer Words

Practice reading these words from בְּרָכוֹת שֶׁל שַׁבָּת.

candle	נֵר
who creates	בּוֹרֵא
the vine	הַגֶּפֶן
who brings forth	הַמּוֹצִיא

Odd Word Out

Read each line and circle the word that does <u>not</u> have a twin.

1. שַׁבָּת שַׁבָּת מוֹדֶה הַמּוֹצִיא מוֹדֶה

2. נֵר לֶחֶם אֲנִי נֵר אֲנִי

3. אֲדָמָה פְּרִי מִן פְּרִי אֲדָמָה

4. מְזוּזָה הַגֶּפֶן מְזוּזָה הַגֶּפֶן הָאָרֶץ

Complete the בְּרָכָה below using the four words you circled.

בָּרוּךְ אַתָּה, יְיָ אֱלֹהֵינוּ, מֶלֶךְ הָעוֹלָם, _____
1

._____ _____ _____
4   3   2

Name two foods we say this בְּרָכָה over. **Hint:** See the picture on page 12.

_____   _____

Draw an apple around each word that means "fruit" in the lines above.
Write your name above each word that means "I."

Use the words in the list below to complete the בְּרָכוֹת.

הַמּוֹצִיא בּוֹרֵא נֵר שַׁבָּת לֶחֶם הַגֶּפֶן

1. בָּרוּךְ אַתָּה, יְיָ אֱלֹהֵינוּ, מֶלֶךְ הָעוֹלָם, אֲשֶׁר
קִדְּשָׁנוּ בְּמִצְוֹתָיו, וְצִוָּנוּ לְהַדְלִיק _____ שֶׁל

_____ .

2. בָּרוּךְ אַתָּה, יְיָ אֱלֹהֵינוּ, מֶלֶךְ הָעוֹלָם, _____
_____ פְּרִי .

3. בָּרוּךְ אַתָּה, יְיָ אֱלֹהֵינוּ, מֶלֶךְ הָעוֹלָם, _____
_____ מִן הָאָרֶץ.

Draw a picture to illustrate the Shabbat item in each blessing above.

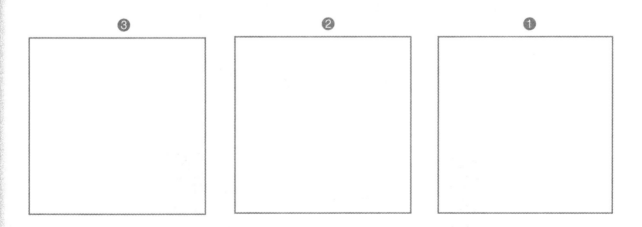

❸   ❷   ❶

Picture Match

Read the words on each line below then circle the word that matches the picture.

1. פְּרִי   לֶחֶם   הַגֶּפֶן   בּוֹרֵא

2. פְּרִי   לֶחֶם   נֵר   הָאָרֶץ

3. נֵר   מוֹדָה   שַׁבָּת   הַמּוֹצִיא

4. מֶלֶךְ   הָאָרֶץ   שַׁבָּת   הַמּוֹצִיא

5. מֶלֶךְ   מִן   בּוֹרֵא   הַגֶּפֶן

6. חַי   וְצִוָּנוּ   מְזוּזָה   תּוֹרָה

7. לַעֲסוֹק   בָּרוּךְ   לֶחֶם   אַתָּה

8. מוֹדָה   מְזוּזָה   בּוֹרֵא   בִּדְבְרֵי

Giving Tzedakah

Many people give צְדָקָה on Friday evening before Shabbat starts. Tzedakah means "justice" or "righteousness." Donating money for צְדָקָה is just one way we can do what is just and right. In what other ways can we fulfill the mitzvah of צְדָקָה?

Let There Be Light

In most cases, first we say a בְּרָכָה and then we do the action. For example, we say the בְּרָכָה over fruit, then eat a pear. Complete the sentences below.

First we say:

בָּרוּךְ אַתָּה, יְיָ אֱלֹהֵינוּ, מֶלֶךְ הָעוֹלָם, אֲשֶׁר קִדְּשָׁנוּ בְּמִצְוֹתָיו וְצִוָּנוּ לִקְבֹּעַ מְזוּזָה.

and then we _____.

First we say:

בָּרוּךְ אַתָּה, יְיָ אֱלֹהֵינוּ, מֶלֶךְ הָעוֹלָם, אֲשֶׁר קִדְּשָׁנוּ בְּמִצְוֹתָיו וְצִוָּנוּ לַעֲסוֹק בְּדִבְרֵי תוֹרָה.

and then we _____.

But...

When we light Shabbat candles, it's the opposite: first we do the action—lighting Shabbat candles—then we say the בְּרָכָה. Why?

Lighting fire—in this case, lighting candles—is the kind of work traditional Jewish law teaches us not to do on Shabbat. Because Shabbat begins the moment we have said the בְּרָכָה over the candles, we light the candles first. Then, we cover our eyes while reciting the blessing so that we won't begin to enjoy the candlelight until *after* we have said the blessing.

Practice reading the blessing over the Shabbat candles.

בָּרוּךְ אַתָּה, יְיָ אֱלֹהֵינוּ, מֶלֶךְ הָעוֹלָם, אֲשֶׁר קִדְּשָׁנוּ בְּמִצְוֹתָיו וְצִוָּנוּ לְהַדְלִיק נֵר שֶׁל שַׁבָּת.

Praised are You, Adonai our God, Ruler of the world, who makes us holy with commandments and commands us to light the Shabbat candles.

Light in Jewish Life

Practice reading each of these blessings recited over candles.

1. בָּרוּךְ אַתָּה, יְיָ אֱלֹהֵינוּ, מֶלֶךְ הָעוֹלָם, אֲשֶׁר קִדְּשָׁנוּ בְּמִצְוֹתָיו וְצִוָּנוּ לְהַדְלִיק נֵר שֶׁל שַׁבָּת.

2. בָּרוּךְ אַתָּה, יְיָ אֱלֹהֵינוּ, מֶלֶךְ הָעוֹלָם, אֲשֶׁר קִדְּשָׁנוּ בְּמִצְוֹתָיו וְצִוָּנוּ לְהַדְלִיק נֵר שֶׁל יוֹם טוֹב.

3. בָּרוּךְ אַתָּה, יְיָ אֱלֹהֵינוּ, מֶלֶךְ הָעוֹלָם, אֲשֶׁר קִדְּשָׁנוּ בְּמִצְוֹתָיו וְצִוָּנוּ לְהַדְלִיק נֵר שֶׁל חֲנֻכָּה.

4. בָּרוּךְ אַתָּה, יְיָ אֱלֹהֵינוּ, מֶלֶךְ הָעוֹלָם, בּוֹרֵא מְאוֹרֵי הָאֵשׁ.

Do you recognize the blessing over Ḥanukkah candles? Write its number here. _____

Now write the Hebrew word for Ḥanukkah. _____

לְהַדְלִיק נֵר
שֶׁל שַׁבָּת

Picture Match

Connect each drawing to its matching description.

symbolizes God's presence
in the sanctuary

makes a miracle known

helps us remember a loved
one who has died

A Story

A story passed down for generations explains that since we bless the candles
and wine first, we cover the ḥallah on the Shabbat table so it will not feel hurt
that it is blessed last.

Write your own explanation about why we light at least two candles on
erev Shabbat.

_____

_____

_____

_____

_____

An Opening Toast

Have you ever been to a wedding where someone proposed a toast or made a speech in honor of the bride and groom?

The קִדּוּשׁ is like an opening toast to God. Before drinking the wine or grape juice on Shabbat and holidays, we recite two בְּרָכוֹת, which together are called the קִדּוּשׁ. The first בְּרָכָה is the blessing over the wine, בּוֹרֵא פְּרִי הַגָּפֶן; the second בְּרָכָה sets the day apart and helps to make it holy. In the next chapter we will study the קִדּוּשׁ for Shabbat in greater detail.

Practice reading the בְּרָכָה over wine.

בָּרוּךְ אַתָּה, יְיָ אֱלֹהֵינוּ, מֶלֶךְ הָעוֹלָם, בּוֹרֵא פְּרִי הַגָּפֶן.

Praised are You, Adonai our God, Ruler of the world,
who creates the fruit of the vine.

Choose another Jewish holiday when we say the קִדּוּשׁ. Write its name in

English here. _____

בּוֹרֵא פְּרִי הַגָּפֶן

The Matter of Manna

Shabbat, like a Jewish wedding, includes a festive meal. Practice reading
הַמּוֹצִיא, the blessing we recite before eating bread or a meal containing bread.

בָּרוּךְ אַתָּה, יְיָ אֱלֹהֵינוּ, מֶלֶךְ הָעוֹלָם, הַמּוֹצִיא
לֶחֶם מִן הָאָרֶץ.

Praised are You, Adonai our God, Ruler of the world, who brings forth
bread from the earth.

On Shabbat many people have two חַלוֹת on their dinner table. Why two חַלוֹת?

The Torah tells us that God provided manna (food from heaven) for the
Israelites, which they gathered daily, when they wandered in the desert for
forty years after leaving Egypt.

On Friday, before Shabbat began, the Israelites received a double portion of
manna so they would not have to gather on Shabbat—the day of rest. We put
two חַלוֹת on our Shabbat table to remember the Exodus from Egypt and the
double portion of manna.

Spot the Difference

The two Hebrew words on each line below are almost the same, but there
is an important difference between them. Read the words in the right-hand
column, then find and circle the additional word part in the left-hand column.
Write the word part you circled in each line.

_____	הַתּוֹרָה	1. תּוֹרָה
_____	הַלֶּחֶם	2. לֶחֶם
_____	הָעֵץ	3. עֵץ
_____	הַמּוֹצִיא	4. מוֹצִיא
_____	הָעוֹלָם	5. עוֹלָם

The word part הַ or הָ means **the**. הַ is always attached to a word.

Two of the words above form a familiar blessing phrase. Write them in the
correct order. _____

Putting It in ConTEXT

The מִצְוָה of celebrating Shabbat is one of the Ten Commandments, which appear in two separate places in the Torah. In each place, the Torah gives a different reason for observing Shabbat.

זָכוֹר אֶת־יוֹם הַשַּׁבָּת לְקַדְּשׁוֹ...כִּי שֵׁשֶׁת־יָמִים עָשָׂה יְיָ
אֶת־הַשָּׁמַיִם וְאֶת־הָאָרֶץ...וַיָּנַח בַּיּוֹם הַשְּׁבִיעִי....

Remember the Shabbat day and keep it holy...for in six days God made the heavens and the earth...and on the seventh day God rested....
(Exodus 20:8-11)

שָׁמוֹר אֶת־יוֹם הַשַּׁבָּת לְקַדְּשׁוֹ...כִּי־עֶבֶד הָיִיתָ בְּאֶרֶץ
מִצְרַיִם וַיֹּצִאֲךָ יְיָ אֱלֹהֶיךָ מִשָּׁם....

Observe the Shabbat day and keep it holy...for you were a slave in the land of Egypt and God brought you out of there....
(Deuteronomy 5:12-15)

Complete the activities below:

1. In each Torah excerpt above circle the words that mean "the Shabbat day."

2. What event is mentioned in the first excerpt? _____

3. What event is mentioned in the second excerpt? _____

4. Why do you think we mention these two events in the קִדּוּשׁ?

_____

 **Did You know?**

The two candles on the Shabbat table remind us of the two commandments: שָׁמוֹר and זָכוֹר.

At the Root

We have learned that most Hebrew words are built on three root letters. The root letters in the word שָׁלוֹם ("peace") are שׁלמ. Words built on this root have **wholeness** or **completeness** as part of their meaning.

Circle the three root letters in שָׁלוֹם (Remember: ם is the way מ appears at the end of a word.)

Do you see a connection among "wholeness," "completeness," and "peace"?

Explain your answer. _____

_____

Language Link

Shabbat is the perfect time to express our love for our family and friends. When the candles are lit and Shabbat has begun, we wish each other שַׁבָּת שָׁלוֹם, "a peaceful Shabbat." We may greet visitors with the word שָׁלוֹם— "peace." In this way, we help to create שְׁלוֹם בַּיִת, peace—and respect for one another!—at home.

> What other greetings can help show family and friends that you respect them?

Write one way you can help create שְׁלוֹם בַּיִת in your home.

_____

Clue to Cyberspace

Read the Hebrew words below. Which line contains a greeting we use on Shabbat? Write the number here. _____ Use this clue to do a bonus trick in "Batya's Vert Skate" game in Level 4—בְּרָכוֹת שֶׁל שַׁבָּת—on your computer.

1. מוֹדֶה מֶלֶךְ הַמּוֹצִיא הָאֲדָמָה
2. הָעֵץ חַי שַׁבָּת שָׁלוֹם הַגֶּפֶן
3. פֵּרוֹת לֶחֶם נֵר שָׁלוֹם בַּיִת
4. מְזוּזָה צְדָקָה שַׁבָּת פְּרִי

It's easy to stay in touch with your friends who live close by. Perhaps you see them at school or sports practice, or you play video games at each other's houses. But how do you stay in touch with your friends who live far away? Do you text them? Call them? Schedule sleepovers every few months?

How do *you* stay connected?

Saying prayers and blessings such as the קִדּוּשׁ is one way that Jews stay connected. When Ben and Batya, or you and I, lift our קִדּוּשׁ cup, filled to the brim with wine, it connects us to Jews in Italy and South Africa, France and Israel. In fact, for centuries, Jews around the world have recited Kiddush every Shabbat. Its words remind us of the Torah's teaching that our ancestors were freed from slavery in Egypt 3,500 years ago.

Reciting the קִדּוּשׁ and other prayers is one way Jews stay connected. On the Kiddush cup write or draw other ways Jews everywhere are connected.

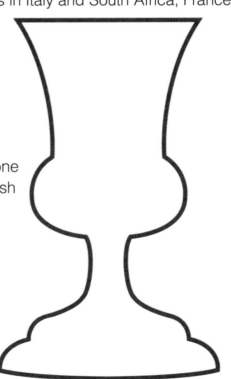

Reciting the Kiddush

The first part of the קִדּוּשׁ begins with a short blessing that you have already learned: בּוֹרֵא פְּרִי הַגָּפֶן.

The second part of the קִדּוּשׁ emphasizes the holiness of Shabbat. In the קִדּוּשׁ we are reminded of two important events. Look ahead to page 42, lines 5 and 7, to find the events, then write them here:

1. _____

2. _____

Read for Speed

With a classmate take turns reading the word parts, words, and phrases in the lines below. Keep practicing until you can both read them fluently.

1. אֲשֶׁר שֶׁר אֲ

2. קִדְּשָׁנוּ נוּ שָׁ דְּ קִ

3. בְּמִצְוֹתָיו תָיו בְּמִצְוֹ מִצְ בְּ

4. בָנוּ נוּ בָ וְרָצָה וְ

5. אֲשֶׁר קִדְּשָׁנוּ בְּמִצְוֹתָיו וְרָצָה בָנוּ

6. וְשַׁבַּת בַּת שַׁ וְ

7. קָדְשׁוֹ שׁוֹ קָדְ

8. בְּאַהֲבָה בָה הֲ אַ בְּ

9. וּבְרָצוֹן רָצוֹן וּבְ

10. הִנְחִילָנוּ לָנוּ חִי הִנְ

11. וְשַׁבַּת קָדְשׁוֹ בְּאַהֲבָה וּבְרָצוֹן הִנְחִילָנוּ

The Kiddush

Practice reading the קִדוּשׁ.

1. בָּרוּךְ אַתָּה, יְיָ אֱלֹהֵינוּ, מֶלֶךְ הָעוֹלָם, בּוֹרֵא פְּרִי הַגָּפֶן.

2. בָּרוּךְ אַתָּה, יְיָ אֱלֹהֵינוּ, מֶלֶךְ הָעוֹלָם,

3. אֲשֶׁר קִדְּשָׁנוּ בְּמִצְוֹתָיו וְרָצָה בָנוּ.

4. וְשַׁבַּת קָדְשׁוֹ בְּאַהֲבָה וּבְרָצוֹן הִנְחִילָנוּ,

5. זִכָּרוֹן לְמַעֲשֵׂה בְרֵאשִׁית.

6. כִּי הוּא יוֹם תְּחִלָּה לְמִקְרָאֵי קֹדֶשׁ,

7. זֵכֶר לִיצִיאַת מִצְרָיִם.

8. כִּי בָנוּ בָחַרְתָּ וְאוֹתָנוּ קִדַּשְׁתָּ מִכָּל הָעַמִּים,

9. וְשַׁבַּת קָדְשְׁךָ בְּאַהֲבָה וּבְרָצוֹן הִנְחַלְתָּנוּ.

10. בָּרוּךְ אַתָּה, יְיָ, מְקַדֵּשׁ הַשַׁבָּת.

1. *Praised are You, Adonai our God, Ruler of the world, who creates the fruit of the vine.*

2. *Praised are You, Adonai our God, Ruler of the world,*

3. *who makes us holy with commandments and takes delight in us.*

4. *In love and favor, God has made the holy Shabbat, our heritage,*

5. *as a memory of the work of creation.*

6. *It is first among our holy days,*

7. *a memory of the going out from Egypt.*

8. *You chose us from all the nations and You made us holy,*

9. *and in (with) love and favor You have given us the Shabbat as a holy inheritance.*

10. *Praised are You, Adonai, who makes the Shabbat holy.*

Practice reading these words from the קִדּוּשׁ.

holiness	קִדּוּשׁ
memory	זִכָּרוֹן
memory	זֵכֶר
(of the) work of creation	(לְ)מַעֲשֵׂה בְרֵאשִׁית
(of the) going out from Egypt	(לְ)יְצִיאַת מִצְרָיִם
(in/with) love	(בְּ)אַהֲבָה
(and in/with) favor	(וּבְ)רָצוֹן

Missing Link

Using the list of words above, the קִדּוּשׁ on page 42, and words you already know, complete the sentences below.

1. זִכָּרוֹן לְמַעֲשֵׂה _____

creation

2. כִּי הוּא יוֹם תְּחִלָּה לְמִקְרָאֵי קֹדֶשׁ _____

a memory

   _____ _____

going out from Egypt

3. וְשַׁבַּת קָדְשְׁךָ _____ _____

and/in with favor   in /with love

הִנְחַלְתָּנוּ

4. _____ אַתָּה, יְיָ, מְקַדֵּשׁ _____.

blessed   the Shabbat

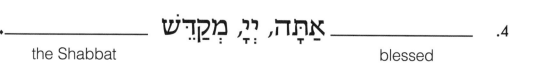

At the Root

You have learned that the קָדוּשׁ reminds us of two important events. Read them below in Hebrew then in English.

‎2. זֵכֶר לִיצִיאַת מִצְרָיִם   ‎1. זִכָּרוֹן לְמַעֲשֵׂה בְרֵאשִׁית

a memory of the going out from Egypt   *a memory of the work of creation*

Underline the first Hebrew word of each phrase.

Circle the three letters that appear in both words. Write the letters. ___ ___ ___

These three letters form the root of the words זִכָּרוֹן and זֵכֶר and tell us that **remember** is part of a word's meaning.

Describe one place, person, or event you remember from when you were young. Why do you think it remains in your memory?

_____

_____

Holiday Link

In the Jewish calendar there is a day on which we remember soldiers who died defending Israel. We call this day יוֹם הַזִּכָּרוֹן, the Day of Remembrance. We observe יוֹם הַזִּכָּרוֹן on the day before יוֹם הָעַצְמָאוּת, Israel's Independence Day.

Name a Jewish holiday that is dedicated to remembering יְצִיאַת מִצְרָיִם.

Write its name in English here. _____

Language Link

In Hebrew a secretary is a מַזְכִּיר (masculine) or a מַזְכִּירָה (feminine).

Circle the three root letters in מַזְכִּירָה and מַזְכִּיר. Write the root. ___ ___ ___

Why do you think מַזְכִּירָה and מַזְכִּיר are built on this root?

The Whole Holy Word

You have learned that the root letters קדשׁ mean **holy** or **set apart**. Look back at the קִדּוּשׁ on page 42 and circle all the words built on the root קדשׁ.

How many words did you circle? _____

Why do you think the קִדּוּשׁ contains so many words having to do with holiness?

_____

_____

Read the blessing below. Then complete the activity that follows.

בָּרוּךְ אַתָּה, יְיָ אֱלֹהֵינוּ, מֶלֶךְ הָעוֹלָם, בּוֹרֵא פְּרִי הַגָּפֶן.

Draw the object we hold when we say this blessing.

Use this clue to reset your timer in the "Kiddush Slingshot" game in Level 5—קִדּוּשׁ—on your computer.

Sometimes saying good-bye can be hard—when your cousin moves away, you leave your camp friends at the end of the summer, or you pack up after visiting your grandparents.

When have you felt sad saying good-bye?

_____

What helped you feel better?

_____

We say good-bye to Shabbat on Saturday evening with a ceremony called הַבְדָּלָה ("separation"), which divides the holiness of Shabbat from the busy week that lies ahead—a week of schoolwork and play dates, soccer practice and guitar lessons, friends to call and IMs to send.

Think About It: What purpose does it serve to have a ceremony that separates Shabbat from the other days of the week?

The Four הַבְדָּלָה Blessings

Shabbat ends and the הַבְדָּלָה ceremony takes place when three stars appear in the sky. הַבְדָּלָה has four blessings: over (1) wine, (2) spices, (3) light of a braided candle, and (4) the separation of Shabbat from the other days of the week. At the end, we wish one another שָׁבוּעַ טוֹב—a good week.

1. WINE

We lift the cup of wine. Practice reading the blessing over the wine.

בָּרוּךְ אַתָּה, יְיָ אֱלֹהֵינוּ, מֶלֶךְ הָעוֹלָם, בּוֹרֵא פְּרִי הַגָּפֶן.

Praised are You, Adonai our God, Ruler of the world, who creates the fruit of the vine.

But we don't drink the wine yet...

2. SPICES

We hold up a mixture of sweet-smelling spices that are usually contained in a silver, wood, or ceramic spice box. Practice reading the blessing we say before smelling the spices.

בָּרוּךְ אַתָּה, יְיָ אֱלֹהֵינוּ, מֶלֶךְ הָעוֹלָם,
בּוֹרֵא מִינֵי בְשָׂמִים.

Praised are You, Adonai our God, Ruler of the world, who creates various kinds of spices.

Now we smell the spices to symbolically give us strength for the coming week and to carry over a bit of Shabbat sweetness.

3. CANDLE

We light a special multi-wicked, braided candle. Practice reading the blessing over the candle.

בָּרוּךְ אַתָּה, יְיָ אֱלֹהֵינוּ, מֶלֶךְ הָעוֹלָם,
בּוֹרֵא מְאוֹרֵי הָאֵשׁ.

Praised are You, Adonai our God, Ruler of the world, who creates the fiery lights.

4. SEPARATING

We lift the cup of wine again and praise Adonai for making many distinctions, or differences, in the world. Practice reading the blessing.

1. בָּרוּךְ אַתָּה, יְיָ אֱלֹהֵינוּ, מֶלֶךְ הָעוֹלָם,

2. הַמַּבְדִּיל בֵּין קֹדֶשׁ לְחוֹל,

3. בֵּין אוֹר לְחֹשֶׁךְ, בֵּין יִשְׂרָאֵל לָעַמִּים,

4. בֵּין יוֹם הַשְּׁבִיעִי לְשֵׁשֶׁת יְמֵי הַמַּעֲשֶׂה.

5. בָּרוּךְ אַתָּה, יְיָ, הַמַּבְדִּיל בֵּין קֹדֶשׁ לְחוֹל.

1. *Praised are You, Adonai our God, Ruler of the world,*

2. *who separates the holy from the everyday,*

3. *light from darkness, Israel from the other nations,*

4. *the seventh day from the six days of work.*

5. *Praised are You, Adonai, who separates the holy from the everyday.*

Now we drink almost the entire cup of wine and then extinguish the flame of the candle in what remains.

Circle the word בֵּין ("between") each time it appears in the blessing. Now read each phrase in which בֵּין appears. Circle the phrase that you read twice.

To conclude the הַבְדָּלָה ceremony, friends and family join hands and wish each other שָׁבוּעַ טוֹב — a good week!

Why do you think friends and family join hands during Havdalah?

Language Link

In Hebrew, the word שָׁבוּעַ means "week." Read the clue below then guess what the holiday name שָׁבוּעוֹת means: _____

Clue: There are seven weeks from פֶּסַח, which marks the Israelites' escape from Egypt, to the beginning of שָׁבוּעוֹת, which celebrates the Israelites' receiving the Ten Commandments at Mount Sinai.

Prayer Words

Practice reading these words from הַבְדָלָה.

spices	בְּשָׂמִים
fire	אֵשׁ
who separates	הַמַּבְדִּיל
holy	קֹדֶשׁ
everyday	חוֹל

Circle the prayer word above that is built on the same root letters as the word
הַבְדָלָה. What does הַבְדָלָה mean? _____

Draw a line to join the two parts of each הַבְדָלָה word.

דֶשׁ	בְּשָׂ	.1
מִים	שָׂ	.2
בוּעַ	קֹ	.3
ל	אֵ	.4
דָלָה	חוֹ	.5
שׁ	הַבְ	.6

Draw the following:

A flame next to the beginning of the word that means "fire."

A spice box next to the word that means "spices."

A calendar next to the word that means "week."

49

A Secret Word

Read each statement below. If it is correct, circle the letter in the כֵּן column. If it is incorrect, circle the letter in the לֹא column.

	לֹא	כֵּן
1. We say בּוֹרֵא פְּרִי הַגָּפֶן over spices.	ב	ג
2. We say שָׁבוּעַ טוֹב to welcome שַׁבָּת on Friday night.	שׁ	ת
3. During הַבְדָּלָה we light a multi-wicked candle.	ז	מ
4. The הַבְדָּלָה ceremony takes place on Shabbat morning.	י	ב
5. הַבְדָּלָה means "separation."	א	ס

Copy the letters you circled. ____ ____ ____ ____ ____
  5   4   3   2   1

What does this word mean? _____

בּוֹרֵא מִינֵי בְשָׂמִים

Making "Sense" of הַבְדָּלָה

In the הַבְדָּלָה ceremony we use all of our senses.

Use the words below to fill in the blanks in the sentence.

smell   **taste**   **see**   **hear**   **touch**

During הַבְדָּלָה, we _____ the wine, _____ the fragrant spices, _____ the dancing flames, _____ the words of the blessing, and _____ family and friends as we wish them שָׁבוּעַ טוֹב.

Now write the number of each blessing or Hebrew expression under the picture that depicts the sense we use.

_____   _____   _____   _____   _____

1. בָּרוּךְ אַתָּה, יְיָ אֱלֹהֵינוּ, מֶלֶךְ הָעוֹלָם, בּוֹרֵא פְּרִי הַגָּפֶן.

2. בָּרוּךְ אַתָּה, יְיָ אֱלֹהֵינוּ, מֶלֶךְ הָעוֹלָם, בּוֹרֵא מִינֵי בְשָׂמִים.

3. בָּרוּךְ אַתָּה, יְיָ אֱלֹהֵינוּ, מֶלֶךְ הָעוֹלָם, בּוֹרֵא מְאוֹרֵי הָאֵשׁ.

4. בָּרוּךְ אַתָּה, יְיָ אֱלֹהֵינוּ, מֶלֶךְ הָעוֹלָם, הַמַּבְדִּיל בֵּין קֹדֶשׁ לְחוֹל, בֵּין אוֹר לְחשֶׁךְ, בֵּין יִשְׂרָאֵל לָעַמִּים, בֵּין יוֹם הַשְּׁבִיעִי לְשֵׁשֶׁת יְמֵי הַמַּעֲשֶׂה. בָּרוּךְ אַתָּה, יְיָ, הַמַּבְדִּיל בֵּין קֹדֶשׁ לְחוֹל.

5. "שָׁבוּעַ טוֹב."

Why do you think we use all five senses during הַבְדָּלָה?

Elijah the Prophet

Some people sing a song about Elijah the Prophet at the end of the
הַבְדָּלָה ceremony.

Jewish tradition teaches us that Elijah, who fought for justice and the rights of
the poor, is a messenger of good news and will bring peace to the world.

Can you think of another occasion when we acknowledge Elijah?
Describe it here.

_____

_____

Read the words of the song about Elijah the Prophet—אֵלִיָּהוּ הַנָּבִיא.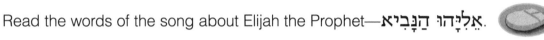

1. אֵלִיָּהוּ הַנָּבִיא

2. אֵלִיָּהוּ הַתִּשְׁבִּי

3. אֵלִיָּהוּ הַגִּלְעָדִי

4. בִּמְהֵרָה בְיָמֵינוּ יָבוֹא אֵלֵינוּ

5. עִם מָשִׁיחַ בֶּן דָּוִד.

1. *Elijah the Prophet*
2. *Elijah the Tishbite*
3. *Elijah from Gilad*
4. *Quickly in our days he will come to us*
5. *with Messiah, son of David.*

Did You know?

During הַבְדָּלָה, after saying the blessing over the candle, we look at the shadows on our fingernails and palms that are created by the light. Just as our fingernails are always growing, so we hope to grow in our own knowledge—every day of our lives.

Write your own explanation about why we examine our fingernails and palms in the light of the הַבְדָּלָה candle.

_____

_____

Clue to Cyberspace

Three of the four pairs below are opposites. Read the words aloud, then write the number of the pair that is *not* made up of opposites. _____

Use this clue to score bonus points in the "Ping Pong" game in Level 6— הַבְדָּלָה —on your computer.

Clue: Look back at the blessing on page 48 for the meanings.

חֹשֶׁךְ/אוֹר .1

חוֹל/קֹדֶשׁ .2

בְּשָׂמִים/אֵשׁ .3

יוֹם הַשְּׁבִיעִי/שֵׁשֶׁת יְמֵי הַמַּעֲשֶׂה .4

$\mathcal{S}$ome people think of food when they think of the Jewish holidays. Ben's favorites are apples and honey, and potato latkes and apple sauce. Batya likes gefilte fish and ḥaroset, blintzes and cheese cake.

What is your favorite Jewish holiday food? _____

There are blessings for each holiday—from Rosh Hashanah and Yom Kippur, to Sukkot and Simḥat Torah, Ḥanukkah, Purim, Pesaḥ, and Shavuot. Some are blessings over food, while others are for lighting the candles, blowing the shofar, or hearing the megillah reading.

Rosh Hashanah רֹאשׁ הַשָּׁנָה

On רֹאשׁ הַשָּׁנָה we celebrate the creation of the world and the beginning of a new Jewish year. By dipping apples in honey and saying the בְּרָכָה over fruit, we ask God to give us a sweet new year. We wish each other a good and sweet new year:

What can you do to make the year sweeter in your home?

שָׁנָה טוֹבָה וּמְתוּקָה

Practice reading the בְּרָכָה over fruit.

בָּרוּךְ אַתָּה, יְיָ אֱלֹהֵינוּ, מֶלֶךְ הָעוֹלָם, בּוֹרֵא פְּרִי הָעֵץ.

Praised are You, Adonai our God, Ruler of the world,
who creates the fruit of the tree.

On רֹאשׁ הַשָּׁנָה, Batya and Ben fulfill the מִצְוָה of hearing the שׁוֹפָר sounded.

Practice reading the בְּרָכָה שֶׁל מִצְוָה we say before we blow the שׁוֹפָר or hear it sounded.

בָּרוּךְ אַתָּה, יְיָ אֱלֹהֵינוּ, מֶלֶךְ הָעוֹלָם, אֲשֶׁר קִדְּשָׁנוּ
בְּמִצְוֹתָיו וְצִוָּנוּ לִשְׁמֹעַ קוֹל שׁוֹפָר.

*Praised are You, Adonai our God, Ruler of the world, who makes us holy
with commandments and commands us to hear the sound of the shofar.*

Circle the Hebrew word for "shofar" in the blessing.

Prayer Words

Practice reading these words from the Rosh Hashanah blessing.

to hear	לִשְׁמֹעַ
sound, voice	קוֹל
shofar	שׁוֹפָר

Picture Match

Draw a line to connect the word to its matching picture.

שׁוֹפָר

לִשְׁמֹעַ

קוֹל

At the Root

Do you know the prayer called the שְׁמַע?

שְׁמַע יִשְׂרָאֵל יְיָ אֱלֹהֵינוּ יְיָ אֶחָד.

The first word, שְׁמַע, means "hear." (The whole line means "Hear, O Israel, Adonai is our God, Adonai is One.") Look again at the word לִשְׁמֹעַ in Prayer Words on page 55. What does לִשְׁמֹעַ mean? _____

שְׁמַע and לִשְׁמֹעַ are built on the same three root letters. Write the root here:

_____ _____ _____

What is the general English meaning of these words? _____

It's a First

Think of something new you just bought or something you did recently for the first time.

What was it? _____

There is a special בְּרָכָה we say when we do something for the first time, on the first days of a holiday, or when we reach a new stage in our lives. The בְּרָכָה is called שֶׁהֶחֱיָנוּ. On רֹאשׁ הַשָּׁנָה we say שֶׁהֶחֱיָנוּ after lighting the holiday candles, after reciting the holiday קִדּוּשׁ, and before hearing the שׁוֹפָר for the first time. The blessing thanks God for giving us life and allowing us to reach this special moment in time.

Practice reading שֶׁהֶחֱיָנוּ.

בָּרוּךְ אַתָּה, יְיָ אֱלֹהֵינוּ, מֶלֶךְ הָעוֹלָם, שֶׁהֶחֱיָנוּ, וְקִיְּמָנוּ, וְהִגִּיעָנוּ לַזְּמַן הַזֶּה.

Praised are you, Adonai our God, Ruler of the world, who has given us life, sustained us, and enabled us to reach this time.

סֻכּוֹת Sukkot

One of Batya and Ben's favorite holidays is סֻכּוֹת, an autumn harvest festival. A סֻכָּה is a booth or hut. It reminds us that 3,500 years ago the Israelites left Egypt and wandered in the desert for forty years, living in huts, before reaching the Land of Israel. It also reminds us of Jewish farmers in ancient Israel who built סֻכּוֹת in their fields during the harvest.

Because Sukkot is a harvest holiday, many people decorate their סֻכּוֹת with autumn fruits and vegetables. Using crayons or colored pencils, turn each Hebrew letter below into a drawing of one of your favorite fruits or vegetables.

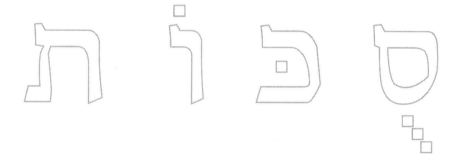

It is a mitzvah to sit in a סֻכָּה. Practice reading the בְּרָכָה we say in the סֻכָּה:

בָּרוּךְ אַתָּה, יְיָ אֱלֹהֵינוּ, מֶלֶךְ הָעוֹלָם, אֲשֶׁר קִדְּשָׁנוּ בְּמִצְוֹתָיו וְצִוָּנוּ לֵישֵׁב בַּסֻּכָּה.

Praised are you, Adonai our God, Ruler of the world, who makes us holy with commandments and commands us to sit in the sukkah.

On סֻכּוֹת it is a mitzvah to shake a לוּלָב together with an אֶתְרוֹג.

Practice reading the בְּרָכָה we say over the לוּלָב and אֶתְרוֹג.

בָּרוּךְ אַתָּה, יְיָ אֱלֹהֵינוּ, מֶלֶךְ הָעוֹלָם, אֲשֶׁר קִדְּשָׁנוּ בְּמִצְוֹתָיו וְצִוָּנוּ עַל נְטִילַת לוּלָב.

Praised are you, Adonai our God, Ruler of the world, who makes us holy with commandments and commands us to lift up the lulav.

What is the clue that these are בְּרָכוֹת שֶׁל מִצְוָה?

Prayer Words

Practice reading these words from the Sukkot blessings.

in the sukkah	בַּסֻּכָּה
lulav	לוּלָב
etrog	אֶתְרוֹג

Picture Match

Fill in the missing Hebrew word that matches the picture.

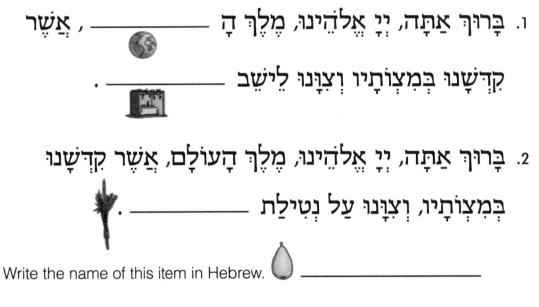

1. בָּרוּךְ אַתָּה, יְיָ אֱלֹהֵינוּ, מֶלֶךְ הָ _____ , אֲשֶׁר

קִדְּשָׁנוּ בְּמִצְוֹתָיו וְצִוָּנוּ לֵישֵׁב _____ .

2. בָּרוּךְ אַתָּה, יְיָ אֱלֹהֵינוּ, מֶלֶךְ הָעוֹלָם, אֲשֶׁר קִדְּשָׁנוּ

בְּמִצְוֹתָיו, וְצִוָּנוּ עַל נְטִילַת _____ .

Write the name of this item in Hebrew. _____

Coded Invitation

Along with family and friends, we symbolically invite *ushpizin*, biblical ancestors, to visit our סֻכָּה.

Can you figure out which *ushpizin* are coming to visit Batya and Ben in their סֻכָּה? Write their names in English.

מִרְיָם	שָׂרָה	מֹשֶׁה	אַבְרָהָם
_____	_____	_____	_____

רוּת	יוֹסֵף	דָּוִד
_____	_____	_____

Ḥanukkah חֲנֻכָּה

On the eight days of חֲנֻכָּה, Batya and Ben spin dreidels, eat crispy potato latkes, exchange gifts, and light candles in the חֲנֻכִּיָּה. They say the following בְּרָכוֹת on this Festival of Lights.

Practice reading the first blessing over the Ḥanukkah candles.

בָּרוּךְ אַתָּה, יְיָ אֱלֹהֵינוּ, מֶלֶךְ הָעוֹלָם, אֲשֶׁר קִדְּשָׁנוּ בְּמִצְוֹתָיו וְצִוָּנוּ לְהַדְלִיק נֵר שֶׁל חֲנֻכָּה.

Praised are you, Adonai our God, Ruler of the world, who makes us holy with commandments and commands us to light the Ḥanukkah candles.

The second blessing praises God for making miracles.

בָּרוּךְ אַתָּה, יְיָ אֱלֹהֵינוּ, מֶלֶךְ הָעוֹלָם, שֶׁעָשָׂה נִסִּים לַאֲבוֹתֵינוּ בַּיָּמִים הָהֵם בַּזְּמַן הַזֶּה.

Praised are you, Adonai our God, Ruler of the world, who made miracles for our ancestors in those days, at this time.

What miracle did God make for our ancestors?

_____

Describe a wonderful event (something like a miracle) that happened in your own life.

_____

On the first night of Ḥanukkah, we recite a third blessing thanking God for allowing us to celebrate the holiday once again.

בָּרוּךְ אַתָּה, יְיָ אֱלֹהֵינוּ, מֶלֶךְ הָעוֹלָם, שֶׁהֶחֱיָנוּ, וְקִיְּמָנוּ, וְהִגִּיעָנוּ לַזְּמַן הַזֶּה.

Praised are you, Adonai our God, Ruler of the world, who has given us life, sustained us, and enabled us to reach this time.

Circle the word in the blessing that is also its name.

Prayer Words

Practice reading these words from the Ḥanukkah blessings.

Ḥanukkah   חֲנֻכָּה

miracles   נִסִּים

at this time   בַּזְּמַן הַזֶּה

The Hebrew letters on a dreidel—נגהש—stand for

נֵס גָּדוֹל הָיָה שָׁם

a great miracle happened there

Circle the Hebrew word for "miracle."

Now write "miracles" in Hebrew. _____

Facing the חֲנֻכִּיָּה, we place the Ḥanukkah candles starting on the right, but we light them from left to right, the newest candle first.

Complete the activities based on the drawings of the חֲנֻכִּיָּה.

Which night of Ḥanukkah is it?

_____

Draw an arrow pointing to the candle we will light first.

Pesah  פֶּסַח

In Ben and Batya's family everyone helps prepare for the seder. Ben washes the parsley and pours the wine. Batya chops haroset and dishes out the bitter herbs. Doug the fish eats matzah crumbs instead of fish food.

In your home, what is your job in preparing for the seder?

Practice reading the blessings we say during the Passover seder.

Drinking the Wine

בָּרוּךְ אַתָּה, יְיָ אֱלֹהֵינוּ, מֶלֶךְ הָעוֹלָם, בּוֹרֵא פְּרִי הַגָּפֶן.

Praised are You, Adonai our God, Ruler of the world, who creates the fruit of the vine.

Eating a Green Vegetable

בָּרוּךְ אַתָּה, יְיָ אֱלֹהֵינוּ, מֶלֶךְ הָעוֹלָם, בּוֹרֵא פְּרִי הָאֲדָמָה.

Praised are You, Adonai our God, Ruler of the world, who creates the fruit of the earth.

Eating the Matzah

בָּרוּךְ אַתָּה, יְיָ אֱלֹהֵינוּ, מֶלֶךְ הָעוֹלָם, הַמּוֹצִיא לֶחֶם מִן הָאָרֶץ.

Praised are You, Adonai our God, Ruler of the world, who brings forth bread from the earth.

בָּרוּךְ אַתָּה, יְיָ אֱלֹהֵינוּ, מֶלֶךְ הָעוֹלָם, אֲשֶׁר קִדְּשָׁנוּ בְּמִצְוֹתָיו וְצִוָּנוּ עַל אֲכִילַת מַצָּה.

Praised are you, Adonai our God, Ruler of the world, who makes us holy with commandments and commands us to eat matzah.

Eating Bitter Herbs

בָּרוּךְ אַתָּה, יְיָ אֱלֹהֵינוּ, מֶלֶךְ הָעוֹלָם, אֲשֶׁר קִדְּשָׁנוּ בְּמִצְוֹתָיו וְצִוָּנוּ עַל אֲכִילַת מָרוֹר.

Praised are you, Adonai our God, Ruler of the world, who makes us holy with commandments and commands us to eat bitter herbs.

Practice reading these words from the Pesaḥ blessings.

the earth	הָאֲדָמָה
eating (of)	אֲכִילַת
matzah	מַצָּה
maror/bitter herbs	מָרוֹר

Make a Match

Write the number of each picture next to its matching בְּרָכָה. Then fill in the missing Hebrew word in each בְּרָכָה.

4   3   2   1

‎1. _____ בָּרוּךְ אַתָּה, יְיָ אֱלֹהֵינוּ, מֶלֶךְ הָעוֹלָם,
בּוֹרֵא פְּרִי _____ .

‎2. _____ בָּרוּךְ אַתָּה, יְיָ אֱלֹהֵינוּ, מֶלֶךְ הָעוֹלָם, בּוֹרֵא פְּרִי

_____ .

‎3. _____ בָּרוּךְ אַתָּה, יְיָ אֱלֹהֵינוּ, מֶלֶךְ הָעוֹלָם, אֲשֶׁר
קִדְּשָׁנוּ בְּמִצְוֹתָיו וְצִוָּנוּ עַל אֲכִילַת _____ .

‎4. _____ בָּרוּךְ אַתָּה, יְיָ אֱלֹהֵינוּ, מֶלֶךְ הָעוֹלָם, אֲשֶׁר
קִדְּשָׁנוּ בְּמִצְוֹתָיו וְצִוָּנוּ עַל אֲכִילַת _____ .

Put a check next to the two בְּרָכוֹת שֶׁל מִצְוָה above.

Order of the Seder

The word **סֵדֶר** means "order." We follow a specific *order* in the Haggadah as we retell the events of the Exodus and explain the meaning of the holiday rituals and symbols.

Practice reading the order of the seder (some people sing it to help remember the list!). Then complete the activities that follow.

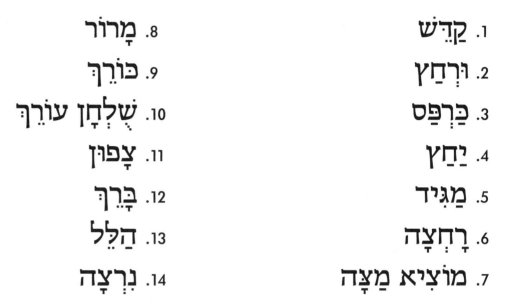

8. מָרוֹר	1. קַדֵּשׁ
9. כּוֹרֵךְ	2. וּרְחַץ
10. שֻׁלְחָן עוֹרֵךְ	3. כַּרְפַּס
11. צָפוּן	4. יַחַץ
12. בָּרֵךְ	5. מַגִּיד
13. הַלֵּל	6. רָחְצָה
14. נִרְצָה	7. מוֹצִיא מַצָּה

Put a triangle △ next to the word that has "bless" at its root. **Hint:** Think of the word **בְּרָכָה**.

Put a star ☆ next to the word that has "holy" at its root. **Hint:** Think of the word **קָדוֹשׁ**.

Put a circle ○ next to the word that means "bitter herbs."

Put a squiggly line ～～～ under the word (or words) that tell us it's time to say the blessings over the matzah. Now recite the blessings over the matzah.

Look at #10. The word **שֻׁלְחָן** means "table." Guess what we do at this part of the seder. (Maybe it's your favorite part!) _____

Fluent Blessing Reading

Read the holiday blessings below. Then, on the blank line at the end of each blessing, write the English name of the holiday on which we recite that blessing.

Put a big star ☆ next to your favorite holiday!

1. בָּרוּךְ אַתָּה, יְיָ אֱלֹהֵינוּ, מֶלֶךְ הָעוֹלָם, אֲשֶׁר קִדְּשָׁנוּ
   בְּמִצְוֹתָיו וְצִוָּנוּ עַל אֲכִילַת מָרוֹר. _____

2. בָּרוּךְ אַתָּה, יְיָ אֱלֹהֵינוּ, מֶלֶךְ הָעוֹלָם, אֲשֶׁר קִדְּשָׁנוּ
   בְּמִצְוֹתָיו וְצִוָּנוּ לֵישֵׁב בַּסֻּכָּה. _____

3. בָּרוּךְ אַתָּה, יְיָ אֱלֹהֵינוּ, מֶלֶךְ הָעוֹלָם, אֲשֶׁר קִדְּשָׁנוּ
   בְּמִצְוֹתָיו וְצִוָּנוּ לִשְׁמֹעַ קוֹל שׁוֹפָר. _____

4. בָּרוּךְ אַתָּה, יְיָ אֱלֹהֵינוּ, מֶלֶךְ הָעוֹלָם, אֲשֶׁר קִדְּשָׁנוּ
   בְּמִצְוֹתָיו וְצִוָּנוּ עַל אֲכִילַת מַצָּה. _____

5. בָּרוּךְ אַתָּה, יְיָ אֱלֹהֵינוּ, מֶלֶךְ הָעוֹלָם, אֲשֶׁר קִדְּשָׁנוּ
   בְּמִצְוֹתָיו וְצִוָּנוּ לְהַדְלִיק נֵר שֶׁל חֲנֻכָּה. _____

6. בָּרוּךְ אַתָּה, יְיָ אֱלֹהֵינוּ, מֶלֶךְ הָעוֹלָם, אֲשֶׁר קִדְּשָׁנוּ
   בְּמִצְוֹתָיו וְצִוָּנוּ עַל מִקְרָא מְגִלָּה. _____

Are you having a good day—יוֹם טוֹב—today? The phrase יוֹם טוֹב also means a Jewish holiday. Why do you think "good day" and "Jewish holiday" are the same in Hebrew?

_____

_____

חַג is another way of saying "holiday." We wish each other חַג שָׂמֵחַ — "happy holiday."

Clue to Cyberspace

Find and circle the 15 holiday words or phrases in the lines below. One phrase appears twice. **Hint:** All the words and phrases appear in this chapter.

מָרוֹרמַצָּהשׁוֹפָרחֲנֻכָּהמְגִלָּהיּוֹםטוֹב

חַגשָׂמֵחַמַסְכָּהלוּלָבאֶתְרוֹגסֵדֶר

רֹאשׁהַשָׁנָהֶחַגשָׂמֵחַמַסְכּוֹתפֶּסַח

Which phrase appears twice? Write it here. _____

Use this clue to reset your timer in the "Holiday Slingshot" game in Level 7—בְּרָכוֹת שֶׁל יוֹם טוֹב—on your computer.

Batya has been preparing for the seder by practicing singing the Four Questions—מַה נִּשְׁתַּנָּה—over and over. Have you ever led the singing of מַה נִּשְׁתַּנָּה? If so, how did you feel?

Practice reading, then singing מַה נִּשְׁתַּנָּה.

מַה נִּשְׁתַּנָּה הַלַּיְלָה הַזֶּה מִכָּל הַלֵּילוֹת?

1. שֶׁבְּכָל הַלֵּילוֹת אָנוּ אוֹכְלִין חָמֵץ וּמַצָּה, הַלַּיְלָה הַזֶּה כֻּלּוֹ מַצָּה.

2. שֶׁבְּכָל הַלֵּילוֹת אָנוּ אוֹכְלִין שְׁאָר יְרָקוֹת, הַלַּיְלָה הַזֶּה מָרוֹר.

3. שֶׁבְּכָל הַלֵּילוֹת אֵין אָנוּ מַטְבִּילִין, אֲפִילוּ פַּעַם אֶחָת, הַלַּיְלָה הַזֶּה שְׁתֵּי פְעָמִים.

4. שֶׁבְּכָל הַלֵּילוֹת אָנוּ אוֹכְלִין בֵּין יוֹשְׁבִין וּבֵין מְסֻבִּין, הַלַּיְלָה הַזֶּה כֻּלָּנוּ מְסֻבִּין.

Why is this night different from all other nights?

1. *On all other nights we eat leavened and unleavened bread, but on this night we eat only matzah.*

2. *On all other nights we eat all kinds of herbs, but on this night we eat only bitter herbs.*

3. *On all other nights we do not dip even once, but on this night we dip twice.*

4. *On all other nights we eat either sitting or reclining, but on this night we all recline.*

The Answers

Test your knowledge of Pesaḥ customs by answering the questions מַה נִּשְׁתַּנָּה asks about the seder.

הַלַּיְלָה הַזֶּה כֻּלּוֹ מַצָּה

1. Why do we eat מַצָּה?

_____

הַלַּיְלָה הַזֶּה מָרוֹר

2. Why do we eat מָרוֹר?

_____

הַלַּיְלָה הַזֶּה שְׁתֵּי פְעָמִים

3. What do we dip in salt water? What do we dip in ḥaroset?

_____

הַלַּיְלָה הַזֶּה כֻּלָּנוּ מְסֻבִּין

4. Why do we recline?

_____

אֲכִילַת מַצָּה

Practice reading these words from מַה נִּשְׁתַּנָּה.

(the) night   (הַ)לַּיְלָה

this   הַזֶּה

Language Link

The word part הַ at the beginning of a word usually means "the."
Circle הַ in the words above.

However, when we add הַלַּיְלָה + הַזֶּה, we translate the phrase הַלַּיְלָה הַזֶּה
as "this night."

What night are we referring to here? _____

Can you translate the phrase לַיְלָה טוֹב? **Hint:** You might say this to someone
at bedtime. _____

Challenge: What do you think the phrase בֹּקֶר טוֹב means? **Hint:** It's the
opposite end of the day. _____

בְּכָל דּוֹר וָדוֹר חַיָּב אָדָם
לִרְאוֹת אֶת עַצְמוֹ כְּאִלּוּ
הוּא יָצָא מִמִּצְרַיִם

Me Too!

Describe two things your family does every year at the Pesaḥ seder.

1. _____

2. _____

If you ask a parent or grandparent, you're likely to find that they recited the same or similar words, performed the same rituals, and ate the same foods at their seders when they were young.

Why do you think Jews gather each year to retell the Pesaḥ story and remember our freedom from slavery in Egypt?

_____

_____

The Haggadah tells us:

בְּכָל־דּוֹר וָדוֹר חַיָּב אָדָם לִרְאוֹת אֶת־עַצְמוֹ כְּאִלּוּ
הוּא יָצָא מִמִּצְרָיִם.

In every generation it is our duty to see ourselves as if we were freed from slavery in Egypt.

Why do you think it is important to "see ourselves as if we were freed from slavery in Egypt"?

_____

_____

The theme of our being freed from slavery in Egypt occurs in many prayers. Write in Hebrew the name of the prayer in which this phrase appears:

זֵכֶר לִיצִיאַת מִצְרָיִם

Hint: We say it over wine on Shabbat and holidays. Look back at Chapter 5.

_____

The Four Children

In the Haggadah we read about four children. Each child relates to the Passover story in a different way.

Child #1: אֶחָד חָכָם

One who is wise

This child is curious and interested in learning more.

Child #2: אֶחָד רָשָׁע

One who is rebellious

This child does not feel part of the Jewish people.

Child #3: אֶחָד תָּם

One who is simple

This child is an innocent child who wants to understand.

Child #4: אֶחָד שֶׁאֵינוֹ יוֹדֵעַ לִשְׁאוֹל

One who does not know how to ask questions

This is a child who has not yet learned how to ask questions.

Label each picture below with its matching Hebrew description.

_____   _____   _____   _____

_____

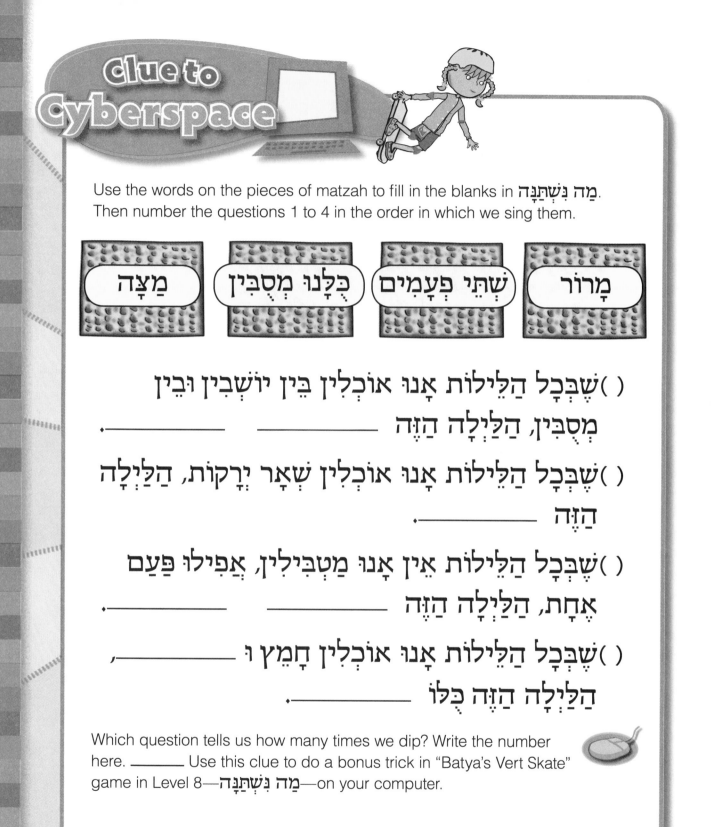

Clue to Cyberspace

Use the words on the pieces of matzah to fill in the blanks in מַה נִּשְׁתַּנָּה.
Then number the questions 1 to 4 in the order in which we sing them.

| מַצָּה | כֻּלָּנוּ מְסֻבִּין | שְׁתֵּי פְּעָמִים | מָרוֹר |

( ) שֶׁבְּכָל הַלֵּילוֹת אָנוּ אוֹכְלִין בֵּין יוֹשְׁבִין וּבֵין
מְסֻבִּין, הַלַּיְלָה הַזֶּה ———— ————.

( ) שֶׁבְּכָל הַלֵּילוֹת אָנוּ אוֹכְלִין שְׁאָר יְרָקוֹת, הַלַּיְלָה
הַזֶּה ————.

( ) שֶׁבְּכָל הַלֵּילוֹת אֵין אָנוּ מַטְבִּילִין, אֲפִילוּ פַּעַם
אֶחָת, הַלַּיְלָה הַזֶּה ———— ————.

( ) שֶׁבְּכָל הַלֵּילוֹת אָנוּ אוֹכְלִין חָמֵץ וּ ————, ————
הַלַּיְלָה הַזֶּה כֻּלּוֹ.

Which question tells us how many times we dip? Write the number
here. ———— Use this clue to do a bonus trick in "Batya's Vert Skate"
game in Level 8—מַה נִּשְׁתַּנָּה—on your computer.

Batya and Ben are preparing trays of macaroni and cheese for a food drive at their synagogue. On Sunday, families in the congregation will deliver the food to a local shelter for homeless people. In addition to giving food, how else can we help people in need?

_____

_____

Saying a blessing before a meal helps us stop and thank God for the food we are about to eat. Saying a blessing *after* a meal—בְּרְכַּת הַמָּזוֹן, also called Grace after Meals—helps us stop and thank God for the food we have just eaten. It also reminds us that both God and people share the task of feeding the world. God provides the food, but it is our responsibility to help feed those who don't have enough.

Is it easier to thank God when you are hungry and you are about to eat a delicious meal, or afterward when you are full and satisfied?

1. בָּרוּךְ אַתָּה, יְיָ אֱלֹהֵינוּ, מֶלֶךְ הָעוֹלָם,

2. הַזָּן אֶת הָעוֹלָם כֻּלּוֹ

3. בְּטוּבוֹ בְּחֵן בְּחֶסֶד וּבְרַחֲמִים.

4. הוּא נוֹתֵן לֶחֶם לְכָל בָּשָׂר

5. כִּי לְעוֹלָם חַסְדּוֹ.

6. וּבְטוּבוֹ הַגָּדוֹל תָּמִיד לֹא חָסַר לָנוּ,

7. וְאַל יֶחְסַר לָנוּ מָזוֹן לְעוֹלָם וָעֶד

8. בַּעֲבוּר שְׁמוֹ הַגָּדוֹל,

9. כִּי הוּא אֵל זָן וּמְפַרְנֵס לַכֹּל

10. וּמֵטִיב לַכֹּל, וּמֵכִין מָזוֹן

11. לְכָל בְּרִיּוֹתָיו אֲשֶׁר בָּרָא.

12. בָּרוּךְ אַתָּה, יְיָ, הַזָּן אֶת הַכֹּל.

1. *Praised are You, Adonai, our God, Ruler of the world,*
2. *Who feeds the entire world*
3. *with goodness, with grace, with kindness and with mercy.*
4. *You give bread to all people,*
5. *for Your kindness lasts forever.*
6. *Because of Your great goodness we have never lacked food,*
7. *Nor shall we ever lack food in the future*
8. *because of Your great name,*
9. *for You support and assist all creatures*
10. *and bring goodness to all, and provide food*
11. *for all You have created.*
12. *Praised are You, Adonai, who gives food to everyone.*

In Your Own Words

Choose one line from בִּרְכַּת הַמָּזוֹן that praises God, and write it in Hebrew.

_____

Prayer Words

Practice reading these words from בִּרְכַּת הַמָּזוֹן.

who feeds	הַזָּן
(God's) goodness	טוּבוֹ
(with) kindness	(בְּ)חֶסֶד
food	מָזוֹן

Food for Thought

The following two words are similar:

2. מָזוֹן   1. הַזָּן

Write their English meanings: 1. _____ 2. _____

In each Hebrew word, circle the two letters the words have in common.

Now look back at בִּרְכַּת הַמָּזוֹן on page 73. Circle all the words that are similar to הַזָּן and מָזוֹן. How many words did you find? _____

Why do you think בִּרְכַּת הַמָּזוֹן contains so many words with this meaning?

_____

A national Jewish tzedakah organization named Mazon collects money to feed the hungry. Explain why this is an appropriate name for this organization.

_____

Choose a Hebrew phrase from בִּרְכַּת הַמָּזוֹן that might make a good slogan for the organization. Write it here.

_____

It's a Good Thing

We have learned the word טוֹב ("good") in other places in this book. Can you see the similarities between these two words? טוֹבוֹ   טוֹב

Fill in the missing Hebrew word on each line.

1. יוֹם _____ good day

2. לַיְלָה _____ good night

3. שָׁבוּעַ _____ good week

Challenge: What is another meaning for יוֹם טוֹב? _____

Putting It in ConTEXT

The mitzvah of saying בִּרְכַּת הַמָּזוֹן and thanking God after eating a meal is based on the following verse in the Torah.

וְאָכַלְתָּ וְשָׂבָעְתָּ, וּבֵרַכְתָּ אֶת־יְיָ אֱלֹהֶיךָ עַל־הָאָרֶץ
הַטֹּבָה אֲשֶׁר נָתַן־לָךְ.

When you eat and are satisfied, then you shall bless Adonai for the good land that God has given you. (Deuteronomy 8:10)

Complete the following activities based on this quote from the Torah:

• Write the Hebrew word that means "good." _____

• Write the word built on the root ברכ ("bless"). _____

• Write the word that also appears at the end of the מוֹצִיא—the blessing

over bread. _____

At the Root

Look at the first word in the Hebrew verse in "Putting It in ConTEXT" on page 75. Write the Hebrew word here. _____

You have seen this word in different forms before. Read the following two blessings.

1. בָּרוּךְ אַתָּה, יְיָ אֱלֹהֵינוּ, מֶלֶךְ הָעוֹלָם, אֲשֶׁר קִדְּשָׁנוּ בְּמִצְוֹתָיו וְצִוָּנוּ עַל אֲכִילַת מַצָּה.

2. בָּרוּךְ אַתָּה, יְיָ אֱלֹהֵינוּ, מֶלֶךְ הָעוֹלָם, אֲשֶׁר קִדְּשָׁנוּ בְּמִצְוֹתָיו וְצִוָּנוּ עַל אֲכִילַת מָרוֹר.

Circle the word in each blessing above that looks similar to the word you wrote at the top of the page.

All of these words are built on the root letters אכל and have **eat** as part of their meaning.

Complete the following sentence.

We say blessings 1 and 2 at the Pesaḥ _____ when we

eat (1) _____ and (2) _____ .

Come On In!

When was the last time you had guests over to visit? Who came?
What did you do to make them feel welcome?

You fulfilled the mitzvah of הַכְנָסַת אוֹרְחִים —welcoming guests. This mitzvah began in earliest biblical times. Abraham and Sarah—the perfect hosts—invited travellers into their tent and offered them shelter and food. They even offered them water to wash their feet! (Genesis 18:1–8)

In some traditional homes, Jews keep לֶחֶם ("bread") on the table at all times so that all who enter are welcome to eat.

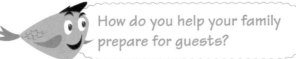

How do you help your family prepare for guests?

Bread, Bread, Bread

Bread is the symbol of food in Jewish life.

Underline the Hebrew word for "bread" in הַמּוֹצִיא.

בָּרוּךְ אַתָּה, יְיָ אֱלֹהֵינוּ, מֶלֶךְ הָעוֹלָם, הַמּוֹצִיא לֶחֶם
מִן הָאָרֶץ.

Write the Hebrew word for bread. _____

Bread is central in many Jewish celebrations.

Connect the bread to the occasion on which we eat it.

רֹאשׁ הַשָּׁנָה

שַׁבָּת

פֶּסַח

All or Nothing

The Hebrew word כֹּל means "all."

Look back at בִּרְכַּת הַמָּזוֹן on page 73 and count how many times
כֹּל, הַכֹּל, כֻּלּוֹ, לַכֹּל and any other variation of these words appear.

Write the number of times here. _____

Reread the English translation of בִּרְכַּת הַמָּזוֹן. Why do you think "all" and
"everyone" appear so many times?

_____

_____

_____

Putting It in ConTEXT

When we read in the Bible of people fulfilling the mitzvah of הַכְנָסַת אוֹרְחִים, "welcoming guests," they often offer their guests bread.

Read the following excerpts from the Torah and circle the Hebrew word for "bread" each time it appears.

1. Abraham and Sarah welcome strangers into their tent:

וְאֶקְחָה פַת־לֶחֶם וְסַעֲדוּ לִבְּכֶם

And let me get you a morsel of bread that you may refresh yourself
(Genesis 18:5)

2. Jethro, Moses's father-in-law, on hearing that an Egyptian—Moses—had helped his daughters water their flock, invited him in to break bread:

קִרְאֶן לוֹ וְיֹאכַל לָחֶם

Call him, so he may eat bread
(Exodus 2:20)

3. God promises Moses that the Israelites will receive manna from the sky while they wander in the wilderness:

וַיֹּאמֶר יְיָ אֶל־מֹשֶׁה, הִנְנִי מַמְטִיר לָכֶם לֶחֶם
מִן־הַשָּׁמָיִם

Adonai said to Moses, "I will cause bread to rain from heaven for you"
(Exodus 16:4)

Clue to Cyberspace

Look back at בְּרְכַּת הַמָּזוֹן on page 73 to help you fill in the missing letters on each line below. Then write the missing letters on the blank lines at the bottom of the page. Use the mystery words to determine which bowl your ball must land in to score bonus points in the "Ping Pong" game in Level 9—בְּרְכַּת הַמָּזוֹן—on your computer.

1. __רוּךְ אַתָּה יְיָ

2. בְּחֵן בְּחֶסֶד וּבְ__חֲמִים

3. הוּא נוֹתֵן לֶחֶם לְ__ל בָּשָׂר

4. הַזָּן אֶ__ הָעוֹלָם כֻּלּוֹ בְּטוּבוֹ

5. וּבְטוּבוֹ __גָּדוֹל

6. תָּ__יד לֹא חָסַר לָנוּ וְאַל יֶחְסַר לָנוּ

7. מָ__וֹן לְעוֹלָם וָעֶד

8. בַּעֲבוּר שְׁמ__ הַגָּדוֹל

9. כִּי הוּא אֵל זָ__ וּמְפַרְנֵס לַכֹּל

Mystery Words:

___ ___ ___ ___ ___   ___ ___ ___ ___

   9   8   7   6   5   4   3   2   1

שְׁמַע 10

What time do you usually go to bed:

on a school night? _____

on the weekend or during vacation? _____

Batya and Ben are in their bedrooms after a long day at school. They recite the שְׁמַע aloud at bedtime and again in the morning. The words of the שְׁמַע come from the Torah.

The שְׁמַע is the Jewish people's simple and complete statement that we believe in the one and only God.

You've probably said the שְׁמַע in the synagogue. Discuss with your classmates: Why do you think we say the שְׁמַע in the synagogue *and* at home?

שְׁמַע יִשְׂרָאֵל

Practice reading the שְׁמַע.

שְׁמַע יִשְׂרָאֵל, יְיָ אֱלֹהֵינוּ, יְיָ אֶחָד.

Hear O Israel, Adonai is our God, Adonai is One.

When you read or recite the שְׁמַע, you are saying, "I am a member of the Jewish people."

Many people consider the שְׁמַע to be like a Pledge of Allegiance to God. Do you? Why or why not?

_____

_____

Prayer Words

Practice reading these words from the שְׁמַע.

hear	שְׁמַע
Israel	יִשְׂרָאֵל
one	אֶחָד

Unscramble the Prayer

The six words of the שְׁמַע are mixed up. Number them in the correct order.

שְׁמַע   אֶחָד   יְיָ   אֱלֹהֵינוּ יִשְׂרָאֵל   יְיָ

◯   ◯   ◯   ◯   ◯   ◯

Putting It in ConTEXT

Before the time of our biblical ancestors, people believed in many gods. Some prayed to idols. Who was the first person to believe in one God?

Write his name in Hebrew here. _____

Hint: Look back at page 8.

Judaism brought a new idea of God to the world. Judaism taught that there is only one God —יְיָ אֶחָד— and that God is the Creator of everything. In the Ten Commandments we read:

לֹא-יִהְיֶה לְךָ אֱלֹהִים אֲחֵרִים עַל-פָּנָי.

You shall have no other gods besides me.
(Exodus 20:3 and Deuteronomy 5:7)

Why do you think "gods" is written with a lowercase g?

_____

Kavanah

Because the שְׁמַע is so important, we try to say it with deep concentration, also called כַּוָּנָה. Many people cover their eyes to block out distractions and to help them focus on the words of the prayer.

Sometimes it's hard to say the שְׁמַע and other prayers with כַּוָּנָה. It can feel as if we are just stringing words together. Sometimes we have to try very hard to put our heart into what we are saying.

Did you know that some people hold up three fingers to cover their eyes when saying the שְׁמַע? What letter does that resemble? Write it here. _____

Hint: This letter reminds us of the name of the prayer. It also reminds us of one of the names we use for God: שַׁדַּי.

What's in a Name?

וַיֹּאמֶר לֹא יַעֲקֹב יֵאָמֵר עוֹד שִׁמְךָ כִּי אִם־יִשְׂרָאֵל

Your name shall no longer be Jacob, but Yisrael

(Genesis 32:29)

In the Torah we read how Jacob wrestled all night with an angel, who in the morning renamed Jacob יִשְׂרָאֵל ("struggled with God"). Ever since then, we have considered ourselves בְּנֵי יִשְׂרָאֵל, the children of Israel.

Read the names with יִשְׂרָאֵל.

Children of Israel	בְּנֵי יִשְׂרָאֵל
State of Israel	מְדִינַת יִשְׂרָאֵל
Nation (People) of Israel	עַם יִשְׂרָאֵל
Land of Israel	אֶרֶץ יִשְׂרָאֵל

Which יִשְׂרָאֵל do you think שְׁמַע יִשְׂרָאֵל refers to? Explain your answer.

_____

The Jewish people have an expression that all of יִשְׂרָאֵל is responsible for one another:

כָּל יִשְׂרָאֵל עֲרֵבִים זֶה בָּזֶה.

Look on the front cover of this book. Write its title. _____

Why do you think that title was chosen for this book?

_____

_____

In what ways is your family responsible for one another?

More about God's Name

אֵל is a Hebrew word for God.

Find and circle the word that means God within the following word: יִשְׂרָאֵל

Now find and circle the word that means God within the following names.

אֱלִישֶׁבַע   רְפָאֵל   מִיכָאֵל   אֱלִימֶלֶךְ   אֱלִירָן

Practice reading the prayer phrases below. Circle the word for God in each.

1. וְהוּא אֵלִי וְחַי גּוֹאֲלִי

2. אֵל מָלֵא רַחֲמִים

3. אֵל רָם וְנִשָּׂא

4. הוּא אֵל זָן וּמְפַרְנֵס לַכֹּל

Language Link

Ben and Batya's names are the same in Hebrew and English! In Hebrew their names are written בֵּן and בַּתְיָה. (Batya's name has another of God's names in it too— יָה! Her name means "daughter of God." Ben's name just means "son"!)

In Hebrew, "name" is שֵׁם. We ask a boy his name by saying: מַה שִׁמְךָ?

We ask a girl her name by saying: מַה שְׁמֵךְ?

Boys *and* girls answer: שְׁמִי _____

If you have a Hebrew name, write it on the blank line above. Otherwise, write your English name.

Now read the second line of the שְׁמַע (you'll learn more about it next year!). Circle the Hebrew word for "name."

בָּרוּךְ שֵׁם כְּבוֹד מַלְכוּתוֹ לְעוֹלָם וָעֶד.

Word Search

In the Word Search, find and circle the words that answer the questions below. Words can run horizontally or diagonally from right to left.

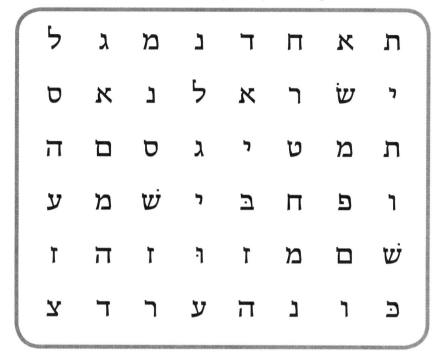

ל	ג	מ	נ	ד	ח	א	ת
ס	א	נ	ל	א	ר	שׁ	י
ה	ם	ס	ג	י	ט	מ	ת
ע	מ	שׁ	י	ב	ח	פ	ו
ז	ה	ז	וּ	ז	מ	ם	שׁ
צ	ד	ר	ע	ה	נ	ו	כּ

1. Which Hebrew word means "hear"?

2. Upon entering a Jewish home, where would you find the שְׁמַע?

3. Which word in the שְׁמַע tells us that we do not believe in many gods?

4. Which people does the שְׁמַע address?

5. When we say the שְׁמַע, we pray with _____ to show our devotion to God.

6. Which one of God's names can we find in the word יִשְׂרָאֵל?

7. Which Hebrew word means "name"?

8. Which word is repeated twice in the שְׁמַע?

Personal Prayer Wrap-Up

In this book we have learned blessings and prayers that express our thanks to God for what we have and what we are able to do. Think back to a typical day this week. What did you learn? What did you accomplish? What were you grateful for? Reflect on that day and write a prayer that expresses your thoughts and feelings.

God, today/on _____ day, I _____

_____ .

It made me feel _____ because _____

_____

_____ .

So I wanted to say _____

_____

_____

_____

_____ .

I hope _____

_____ .

_____

Your name here

What did you do to add shalom, peace, to your home?

In Hebrew, each letter also has a numerical value—א is equal to one, ב is equal to two, and so on. There's even a system—called *gematria*—of interpreting a Hebrew word by adding up the value of its letters. For example, the letters in the word חַי ("live")— ח (8) and י (10)—add up 18. That's why we often give monetary gifts at Jewish celebrations in multiples of 18.

Use the numerical values of the Hebrew letters to figure out the answer to the following mystery question.

Mystery Question:

Which prayer do we put inside a מְזוּזָה?

Find the answer by filling in the matching letter on the blank line below each number at the bottom of this activity. What does the last word mean in English? _____ Use this clue to do a bonus trick in "Batya's Vert Skate" game in Level 10—שְׁמַע—on your computer.

ט	ח	ז	ו	ה	ד	ג	ב	א
9	8	7	6	5	4	3	2	1

צ	פ	ע	ס	נ	מ	ל	כ	י
90	80	70	60	50	40	30	20	10

ת	ש	ר	ק
400	300	200	100

30 1 200 300 10   70 40 300 ◄ START

___ ___ ___ ___ ___   ___ ___ ___

4 8 1   10 10   6 50 10 5 30 1   10 10

___ ___ ___   ___ ___   ___ ___ ___ ___ ___ ___   ___ ___

Number It

Choose a Hebrew word you have learned in this book and write it using the *numbers* that correspond to the Hebrew letters in the word. Remember to write the numbers from right to left. Challenge a classmate to figure out your Hebrew word!

Wrap It Up!

Fun Prayer Activities
Blessing Bee

Choose a partner. Take turns reading each blessing and naming the occasion on which we recite it. If you read the blessing correctly, put a ✓ next to the blessing. Add a second ✓ if you also name the correct occasion.

1. ___ בָּרוּךְ אַתָּה, יְיָ אֱלֹהֵינוּ, מֶלֶךְ הָעוֹלָם, אֲשֶׁר קִדְּשָׁנוּ בְּמִצְוֹתָיו וְצִוָּנוּ עַל אֲכִילַת מַצָּה.

2. ___ בָּרוּךְ אַתָּה, יְיָ אֱלֹהֵינוּ, מֶלֶךְ הָעוֹלָם, שֶׁהֶחֱיָנוּ, וְקִיְּמָנוּ, וְהִגִּיעָנוּ, לַזְּמַן הַזֶּה.

3. ___ בָּרוּךְ אַתָּה, יְיָ אֱלֹהֵינוּ, מֶלֶךְ הָעוֹלָם, אֲשֶׁר קִדְּשָׁנוּ בְּמִצְוֹתָיו וְצִוָּנוּ לִקְבֹּעַ מְזוּזָה.

4. ___ בָּרוּךְ אַתָּה, יְיָ, הַזָּן אֶת הַכֹּל.

5. ___ בָּרוּךְ אַתָּה, יְיָ אֱלֹהֵינוּ, מֶלֶךְ הָעוֹלָם, אֲשֶׁר קִדְּשָׁנוּ בְּמִצְוֹתָיו וְצִוָּנוּ לֵישֵׁב בַּסֻּכָּה.

6. ___ בָּרוּךְ אַתָּה, יְיָ אֱלֹהֵינוּ, מֶלֶךְ הָעוֹלָם, בּוֹרֵא מִינֵי מְזוֹנוֹת.

7. ___ בָּרוּךְ אַתָּה, יְיָ אֱלֹהֵינוּ, מֶלֶךְ הָעוֹלָם, אֲשֶׁר קִדְּשָׁנוּ בְּמִצְוֹתָיו וְצִוָּנוּ לִשְׁמֹעַ קוֹל שׁוֹפָר.

8. ____ בָּרוּךְ אַתָּה, יְיָ, מְקַדֵּשׁ הַשַּׁבָּת.

9. ____ בָּרוּךְ אַתָּה, יְיָ אֱלֹהֵינוּ, מֶלֶךְ הָעוֹלָם, אֲשֶׁר קִדְּשָׁנוּ בְּמִצְוֹתָיו וְצִוָּנוּ לְהַדְלִיק נֵר שֶׁל שַׁבָּת.

10. ____ בָּרוּךְ אַתָּה, יְיָ אֱלֹהֵינוּ, מֶלֶךְ הָעוֹלָם, שֶׁעָשָׂה נִסִּים לַאֲבוֹתֵינוּ בַּיָּמִים הָהֵם בַּזְּמַן הַזֶּה.

11. ____ בָּרוּךְ אַתָּה, יְיָ אֱלֹהֵינוּ, מֶלֶךְ הָעוֹלָם, אֲשֶׁר קִדְּשָׁנוּ בְּמִצְוֹתָיו וְצִוָּנוּ לַעֲסוֹק בְּדִבְרֵי תוֹרָה.

12. ____ בָּרוּךְ אַתָּה, יְיָ אֱלֹהֵינוּ, מֶלֶךְ הָעוֹלָם, בּוֹרֵא מְאוֹרֵי הָאֵשׁ.

לַעֲסוֹק בְּדִבְרֵי
תוֹרָה

Rap-a-Rhythm

Use your pencil to beat a rhythm on the drums as you read these *sound-alike* sets of letters.

Now use your feet to tap as you read the sounds of these *look-alike* sets of letters. Be careful—some letters in a set sound the same, some sound different.

Circle the name of the prayer we recite when we wake up in the morning and thank God for the new day.

מוֹדֶה/מוֹדָה אֲנִי   בִּרְכוֹת שֶׁל יוֹם טוֹב

בִּרְכַּת הַמָּזוֹן

Strike 12!

The numbers on your clock are missing. Read each word to a classmate and, if you read correctly, fill in the missing number. When all the numbers are in place, the clock will strike 12!

בּוֹרֵא

לֶחֶם

וְצִוָּנוּ

הַגָּפֶן

נֵר

מָזוֹן

מִצְוָה

הָעוֹלָם

הַלַּיְלָה

יִשְׂרָאֵל

זִכָּרוֹן

מוֹדֶה

Time It

Complete each prayer phrase by filling in the number of the missing word from the clock on page 91. The first example has been completed for you.

לְהַדְלִיק נֵר שֶׁל חֲנֻכָּה

1. <u>12</u> פְּרִי הָעֵץ

2. בִּרְכוֹת שֶׁל ____

3. ____ אֲנִי לְפָנֶיךָ

4. כָּל ____

5. בּוֹרֵא פְּרִי ____

6. בְּמִצְוֹתָיו ____

7. מַה נִּשְׁתַּנָּה ____ הַזֶּה

8. הַמּוֹצִיא ____ מִן הָאָרֶץ

9. ____ לְמַעֲשֵׂה בְרֵאשִׁית

10. וְאַל יֶחְסַר לָנוּ ____ לְעוֹלָם וָעֶד

11. יְיָ אֱלֹהֵינוּ מֶלֶךְ ____

12. לְהַדְלִיק ____ שֶׁל חֲנֻכָּה

Language Link

Draw a line from each word or phrase in column **א** to its related word or phrase in column **ב**.

ב	**א**
שֵׁם	שְׁלוֹם בַּיִת
בִּרְכוֹת שֶׁל יוֹם טוֹב	תּוֹדָה
שָׁלוֹם	שְׁמִי
שָׁבוּעוֹת	מַזְכִּיר
מוֹדֶה	יוֹם טוֹב
זִכָּרוֹן	שָׁבוּעַ טוֹב

Put a ✓ next to the pair of words that mean "thank."

Write the phrase for "peace at home." _____

It's A Puzzle!

Underline the Hebrew word or phrase that matches the English phrase on each line.

1. God is One   יְיָ אֶחָד   מוֹדֶה אֲנִי   בָּרוּךְ אַתָּה יְיָ

2. the four letters on a dreidel   אבגד   נגהש   חנכה

3. Havdalah spices   בְּשָׂמִים   נֵר   יִשְׂרָאֵל

4. happy holiday   יוֹם טוֹב   קוֹל שׁוֹפָר   חַג שָׂמֵחַ

5. Jewish New Year   סֵדֶר   רֹאשׁ הַשָּׁנָה   פֶּסַח

Batter Up

Play baseball. Try to score a home run by reading all four phrases correctly.

1. הַמַּבְדִּיל בֵּין קֹדֶשׁ לְחוֹל

2. בֵּין אוֹר לְחֹשֶׁךְ

3. בֵּין יִשְׂרָאֵל לָעַמִּים

4. בֵּין יוֹם הַשְּׁבִיעִי לְשֵׁשֶׁת יְמֵי הַמַּעֲשֶׂה

When do we recite these phrases? Hint: The phrases have to do with separation.

_____

Now try to score a home run by reading the four blessings below.

1. בָּרוּךְ אַתָּה, יְיָ אֱלֹהֵינוּ, מֶלֶךְ הָעוֹלָם, בּוֹרֵא פְּרִי
הָאֲדָמָה.

2. בָּרוּךְ אַתָּה, יְיָ אֱלֹהֵינוּ, מֶלֶךְ הָעוֹלָם, הַמּוֹצִיא לֶחֶם
מִן הָאָרֶץ.

3. בָּרוּךְ אַתָּה, יְיָ אֱלֹהֵינוּ, מֶלֶךְ הָעוֹלָם, אֲשֶׁר קִדְּשָׁנוּ
בְּמִצְוֹתָיו וְצִוָּנוּ עַל אֲכִילַת מַצָּה.

4. בָּרוּךְ אַתָּה, יְיָ אֱלֹהֵינוּ, מֶלֶךְ הָעוֹלָם, אֲשֶׁר קִדְּשָׁנוּ
בְּמִצְוֹתָיו וְצִוָּנוּ עַל אֲכִילַת מָרוֹר.

On which holiday do we recite these four blessings? _____

מִלּוֹן

א

earth	אֲדָמָה
one	אֶחָד
eating (of)	אֲכִילַת
God	אֵל
our God	אֱלֹהֵינוּ
Elijah the Prophet	אֵלִיָּהוּ הַנָּבִיא
Amen	אָמֵן
I	אֲנִי
Land of Israel	אֶרֶץ יִשְׂרָאֵל
fire	אֵשׁ
you (for a boy or man)	אַתָּה
etrog	אֶתְרוֹג

ב

(in/with) love	(בְּ)אַהֲבָה
please	בְּבַקָּשָׁה
in the words of	בְּדִבְרֵי
who creates	בּוֹרֵא
at this time	בַּזְּמַן הַזֶּה
(with) kindness	(בְּ)חֶסֶד
with God's commandments	בְּמִצְוֹתָיו
Children of Israel	בְּנֵי יִשְׂרָאֵל
in the sukkah	בַּסֻּכָּה
blessed, praised	בָּרוּךְ
Welcome!	בְּרוּכִים הַבָּאִים
blessing(s)	בְּרָכָה, בְּרָכוֹת
blessing(s) when we do a mitzvah	בְּרָכָה, בְּרָכוֹת שֶׁל מִצְוָה
the blessing after a meal, Grace after Meals	בִּרְכַּת הַמָּזוֹן
spices	בְּשָׂמִים

ה

the	הַ-
the earth	הָאֲדָמָה
separation	הַבְדָּלָה
the vine	הַגֶּפֶן
this	הַזֶּה
who feeds	הַזָּן
welcoming guests	הַכְנָסַת אוֹרְחִים
who separates	הַמַּבְדִּיל
the night	הַלַּיְלָה
who brings forth	הַמּוֹצִיא
the world	הָעוֹלָם

ו

(and in/with) favor	(וּבְ)רָצוֹן
and commands us	וְצִוָּנוּ

ז

remember	זָכוֹר
memory	זֵכֶר
memory	זִכָּרוֹן

ח

holiday	חַג
happy holiday	חַג שָׂמֵחַ
everyday	חוֹל
live, living	חַי
Ḥanukkah	חֲנֻכָּה
Ḥanukkah menorah	חֲנֻכִּיָּה
bridegroom	חָתָן

ט

good	טוֹב
(God's) goodness	טוּבוֹ

י

the Day of Remembrance	יוֹם הַזִּכָּרוֹן
a good day, Jewish holiday	יוֹם טוֹב
Israel's Independence Day	יוֹם הָעַצְמָאוּת
Israel	יִשְׂרָאֵל

ס

| order, Passover seder | סֵדֶר |
| booth(s), hut(s) | סֻכָּה, סֻכּוֹת |

ע

world	עוֹלָם
Nation (People) of Israel	עַם יִשְׂרָאֵל
tree	עֵץ

פ

| fruit(s) | פְּרִי, פֵּרוֹת |

צ

| tzedakah, justice, righteousness | צְדָקָה |

ק

holiness	קִדּוּשׁ
holy	קֹדֶשׁ
makes us holy	קִדְּשָׁנוּ
sound, voice	קוֹל

שׁ

week	שָׁבוּעַ
a good week	שָׁבוּעַ טוֹב
a peaceful Shabbat	שַׁבַּת שָׁלוֹם
God	שַׁדַּי
shofar	שׁוֹפָר
peace, hello, good-bye	שָׁלוֹם
peace in the home	שְׁלוֹם בַּיִת
name	שֵׁם
observe	שָׁמוֹר
my name is...	שְׁמִי
hear	שְׁמַע
a good and sweet New Year	שָׁנָה טוֹבָה וּמְתוּקָה

ת

| thank you | תּוֹדָה |
| Torah | תּוֹרָה |

ב

deep concentration	כַּוָּנָה
all	כֹּל/כָּל
bride	כַּלָּה

ל

lulav	לוּלָב
bread	לֶחֶם
night	לַיְלָה
(of the) going out from Egypt	(ל)יְצִיאַת מִצְרַיִם
(of the) work of creation	(ל)מַעֲשֵׂה בְרֵאשִׁית
to engage	לַעֲסוֹק
to affix	לִקְבֹּעַ
to hear	לִשְׁמֹעַ

מ

State of Israel	מְדִינַת יִשְׂרָאֵל
the Four Questions	מַה נִּשְׁתַּנָּה
What is your name? (to a boy or man)	מַה שְׁמְךָ?
What is your name? (to a girl or woman)	מַה שְׁמֵךְ?
thank, give thanks (boy/man)	מוֹדֶה
thank, give thanks (girl/woman)	מוֹדָה
mezuzah	מְזוּזָה
food	מָזוֹן
secretary (man, woman)	מַזְכִּיר, מַזְכִּירָה
ruler, king	מֶלֶךְ
matzah	מַצָּה
commandment(s)	מִצְוָה, מִצְוֹת
maror/bitter herbs	מָרוֹר

נ

a great miracle happened there	נֵס גָּדוֹל הָיָה שָׁם
miracles	נִסִּים
eternal light	נֵר תָּמִיד
candle, light	נֵר